I0459436

SHADOWS
OVER THE SUN

GISELLE J. ROBIN

ARPress
ILLUMINATING IDEAS.
EMPOWERING VOICES

Copyright © 2020 by Giselle J. Robin.
Cover Design by Francis B.

All rights reserved. No part of this publication may be reproduced, distributed, or transmitted in any form or by any means, including photocopying, recording, or other electronic or mechanical methods, without the prior written permission of the copyright owner and the publisher, except in the case of brief quotations embodied in critical reviews and certain other noncommercial uses permitted by copyright law. For permission requests, write to the publisher, addressed "Attention: Permissions Coordinator," at the address below.

ARPress
45 Dan Road Suite 5
Canton MA 02021

Hotline: 1(800) 220-7660
Fax: 1(855) 752-6001

Ordering Information:
Quantity sales. Special discounts are available on quantity purchases by corporations, associations, and others. For details, contact the publisher at the address above.

Printed in the United States of America.

ISBN-13:   Paperback   979-8-89356-744-1
           eBook   979-8-89356-745-8

Library of Congress Control Number: 2024910685

Giselle J. Robin

To my son, Robert, with love.

CONTENTS

ACKNOWLEDGEMENTS

This book became a reality through the extraordinary support of my friend, Ruth Trigg, who believed in me until I believed in myself.

I also gratefully acknowledge the exceptional care I got—for years of difficult health issues—from my doctor, Feroz Armeerjan.

CHILDHOOD IN WORLD WAR II

-- --

My entry into this world was not exactly what my parents hoped for. I was supposed to be a boy. They registered me as Gisela and I was christened in the Lutheran Church with that name, but my parents called me Peter for the rest of their lives. My father didn't look at me for three months. My mother resented me because of that and also possibly because her father forced her into this marriage while she was engaged to a law student. My father was a widower with a child—my stepsister.

In spite of this negativity, I was a happy child and smiled at everybody.

Soon I had two more sisters, which didn't increase the happiness of my parents. My sister next to me had health issues and needed attention most of the time. I was closer to my youngest sister.

We lived in a comfortable suburb of Hamburg with neighbours like James Last, the musician, and Helmut Schmidt, later Chancellor of Germany and other great people.

Our childhood started in a politically-charged era. Adolf Hitler came into power in 1933. Some people called it a Nazi revolution. The Treaty of Versailles had failed and Germany was in a deep depression. Hitler went on a campaign for change through Germany and Austria. There were few towns of any size where he had not spoken.

He came to know the people first-hand like no other leader ever had. He had a grasp of what could be done by propaganda. His flair knew how to do it, to hold his audience's attention, read their minds, and find sensitive spots to win them over.

Some of his sayings were, 'To be a leader means to move masses'; 'No great idea can be realised into practice without the effective power, which resides in the popular masses'.

Many have described the way he succeeded in communicating passion to his listeners. Men groaned or hissed and women sobbed involuntarily to relieve tension—all caught in the spell of powerful emotions of hatred and exaltation, from which all restraint had been removed.

After deciding on a course of action, Hitler whipped himself into a passion which enabled him to bear down all opposition and provided him with the power to enforce his will on others.

In 1930, inflation was at its highest level. Unemployment had risen to four million.

The economic situation led to hopelessness and anti-semitism, and communism gave him a jump start for his strategy. Many people bought his book *Mein Kampf*, but few read it and less believed it would be followed by action, but industrialists paid Hitler. The impoverished, jobless, politically naïve people in the street were longing for delivery from present evils and were not aware of what was contained in his ideology. When they discovered their fate, it was too late.

After Hitler came to power, unemployment vanished quickly. Art started to flourish. Catchy songs were produced and used in marches, on radios, and in schools. I remember the actors like Greta Garbo, Robert Taylor, Willy Birgel, Heinz Rűhmann, and Marlene Dietrich. Hitler used the arts for propaganda.

The staging of the Olympics in 1936 in Garmisch-Partenkirchen and Berlin, with fifty nations competing, was a huge success for the Germans. The stadium of the Olympic village and sporting grounds were built to impress the world. My mother's youngest brother took part in the games.

In the same year as the Olympics, Wernher von Braun was made head of a secret government project to develop military rockets. He was a relative of my sister's employer. Ferdinand Porsche designed the Volkswagen (VW), the beetle, which became very popular.

A failed army coup in Tokyo forced Japan further towards militarism and fascism, which lead to an anti-communist pact between Germany and Japan, providing mutual support in any war against communist countries.

People started to hope again and were happy, but were soon drawn into new programs like the Hitler Jugend (Hitler Youth) and the Bund Deutscher Mädel (Association of German Girls) for boys and girls over ten years old and into many voluntary services. Many were in despair because they couldn't join the army because they were too young. But there were other formations like the SA (a civil army) and the SS (the 'Elite'). My mother's youngest brother was drawn into the SS because he was tall and very handsome. He was a driving instructor.

Hitler changed the life within our family too. We moved to a new home—one of Hitler's initiatives for big families—in a housing settlement with other similar families. The settlement was surrounded by paddocks on three sides with a lake, where we later learned to swim.

Next to the southerly paddock was a forest. A shooting gallery led through it to some SS quarters. We sneaked into it when there was no guard. It was perfect for playing 'hide and seek'. On the other side of the forest were barracks for the army.

In September 1939, just before the war broke out, my brother was born. Finally, a boy, but he was weak. My father didn't like him because of that. Rations for food were introduced by Hitler early in the war. My brother didn't get any allocation because of his poor health, so we had to share ours with him.

I wanted a baby too and watched my mother nursing him. A few months later, my mother 'gave' him to me. I changed his nappies, fed him, and took him for walks in his pram through the garden under my mother's supervision. I was five years old.

We had a big garden with chickens and rabbits. We collected rabbit food in the paddocks around our place.

My mother did a course for 'master housewives' and was allowed to train girls from rich families to cook and budget, to run a household with children. That was one of Hitler's best ideas. The girls learned what they needed to survive and we learned the lifestyle and manners from the rich. I loved our 'nannies'. The life with them probably formed my wish to live like them one day. My mother was presented in a ceremony with a 'mother cross', which she never wore.

But it was not all rosy. My parents soon became divided about Hitler's surge to power. My father was one of the decent and idealistic people who followed Hitler, while my mother didn't want to be dictated to. There were serious fights between them, sometimes violent, and mum took us to my grandparents several times, which meant we had to change school, where we were not welcome. I ran away from home many times and even felt suicidal at times because of my parents' arguments, but someone in the family always found me after they missed me at meal times.

In good times our mother read stories to us or we sang under the lead of my older sister. Our parents also took us out on bikes through the beautiful countryside with lush paddocks and wheat and rye fields divided by hedges, where we watched and listened to many different birds. Coming home at night, we gazed at the stars and were fascinated by the noiseless flights of owls and bats. Mum had my brother on a seat in the front of the bike and my father pulled a trailer with seats for the girls and food storage underneath. At other times we went to the river Elbe for a swim, the water was still clear then, and sunned ourselves on the white sand. The best times on the river were on New Year's night when the anchored ships sounded their sirens and the bells of all the churches were ringing. We saw the most spectacular fireworks.

Occasionally, there was an outing to the fairground. I went only once with the family and asked mum for a book when they went again. My first book was about a dog called Nicky. I loved reading.

But in spite of mum's emphasis on hygiene, we were often sick and went through most of the childhood illnesses like measles, scarlet fever, diphtheria, whooping cough, pneumonia, and others. We picked it up at school or from other kids in the neighbourhood. When one of us got it, we all followed. My mother was an excellent nurse and always got us back to health quickly with natural resources—mainly hot and cold water treatments and the help of a very knowledgeable naturopath, who made house visits.

The war became more intensive. We heard all about the victories in the Saar region (1935), the invasion of Poland, after a non-aggression pact with Russia. Germany invaded Denmark and Norway in April 1940 and in May 1940 invaded France, Holland, Belgium, and Luxemburg. German forces reached the British Channel after Churchill became Britain's Prime Minister. He declared that 'Britain will never surrender'. France surrendered after German troops marched into Paris.

In this year Germany, Japan, and Italy formed the *Axis alliance-Tripartite* after Germany and Italy had signed the *Pact of steel* in 1939.

When Germany's Luftwaffe started bombing Britain, Russia supplied the fuel. The Germans lost seventy-six aircraft in the first attack. England retaliated by bombing Berlin in August 1940. By that time, thousands of air raid shelters (luftschutz bunkers) were built in the cities of Germany. A bunker was built on the boundary of our and our neighbour's property, which we shared with many neighbours.

We didn't hear much about the losses. Neither did we hear what happened to neighbours or Jews who disappeared. We learned at the end of the war that there were assembly points in Hamburg and other cities, from where Jews were deported to concentration camps. Around 8,000 people were deported from Hamburg. A high percentage of these were Jews with glamorous careers. Jewish business people were accused of swindling their customers (they were reputed to charge enormous interest rates) but were not much different from German business people. When the Jews or anyone else disappeared, there was really no way to find out where they had gone, without endangering oneself. There really was reason to be afraid.

Nazis announced anti-Jewish messages often only in Jewish newspapers to keep the news from the German public and the messages were repressed in other ways. We were told the Jews went to the front, but they never returned. I felt sorry for those people, who were branded with stars and ridiculed or even assaulted. Their houses were smeared with graffiti and sometimes burnt. I was a child. I wanted to help but I didn't understand what was happening.

Things kept getting worse. In February 1941, Hitler sent Rommel with the 'Africa corps' to help Italy in North Africa, where they attacked British Forces.

In April, Germany invaded Yugoslavia and Greece. Yugoslavia surrendered.

In June, Germany invaded Russia (betraying the non-aggression pact, until then Stalin was an ally) with orders of 'maximum cruelty' to civilians, which led to a fanatic resistance.

Hitler made his greatest mistake in July 1941, when he decided to occupy the rich Ukraine and ordered troops to move 'north and south' against the better judgement of the generals.

In all this turmoil, I started primary school. Before we were allowed to enter the school, we had to line up and greet the Führer by lifting the right arm every morning. I wasn't a model student. I earned several punishments from my teacher by hitting me with a ruler on my hands for talking too much—I was bored.

At this time the SS was ordered to prepare the final solution—the plan to murder millions of Europeans: Jews, gypsies, homosexuals, and mentally ill people, communists, Slavs and other 'undesirables' in the numerous concentration camps in Germany, Czechoslovakia, Poland, France and Austria.

In September Hitler resumed the advance to Leningrad and Moscow but the early onset of winter halted his tanks and infantry, who were bogged down by rain and subsequent muds. Even after the mud was frozen they could not advance further than twenty-seven kilometres from Moscow, where they met strong resistance and were pushed back. In December at minus 34ºC, a major Russian counterattack saved Moscow and led to Germany's defeat in Russia.

A day later on 7 December 1941, Japan attacked Pearl Harbour. President Roosevelt had banned all exports of scrap iron, steel, and oil to Japan when Japan started an invasion to China. This action by the US crippled the economy and military in Japan.

The Japanese wanted to expand their empire. They considered that if they destroyed the US Pacific fleet Americans would be demoralised and it could destabilise the American society.

Japan attacked Pearl Harbour without a declaration of war because they wanted to protect their interests in the Dutch colonies, the East Indies, and Malaya, and believed they could defeat the United States. They crippled the US fleet and destroyed Pearl Harbour. The United States joined the war the same day. This marked the turning point of World War II. A few days later, Germany and Italy declared war on the United States.

After the German defeat in Russia in December 1941, Hitler appointed himself as commander in chief of the military. He revealed himself as an ineffective strategist with military campaigns on so many fronts at the same time.

In January 1942, Germany started to sink ships on the US east coast. US troops arrived in Britain and Japan and invaded the Philippines, Indonesia, Malaysia, Burma and the Solomon Islands. Singapore surrendered to Japan in February 1942.

The first major bombing in March 1942 by the British Royal Air Force Bomber Command was conducted against the port of Lubeck by the Air Force Commander Arthur Harris (called 'Bomber' Harris or 'Butcher' Harris). He is claimed to have said, 'Lubeck was built more like a fire lighter than a human habitation' (the buildings were mainly built of wood). In Cologne, Germans experienced carpet bombing in May, when 1,046 bombers dropped 2,000 tons of high explosives. Thousands of civilians died and many more were left homeless. The attack was meant for Hamburg. Hamburg was saved that time by bad weather, but the bombing continued in residential districts of the industrial region of the Ruhr.

US started bombing Tokyo in April. Japan lost its naval superiority in June at the battle of Midway in the Pacific Ocean.

The Germans started a second offensive in Southern Russia in August 1942, facing Stalin's orders: 'No retreats at any costs'. The German advance against Stalingrad was stopped by the Russians' flanking counterattack, which the Germans failed to break. The last German forces in Stalingrad surrendered in February 1943. My favourite uncle was killed in that battle. He was getting married but the wedding papers were lost three times. His bride from Dresden came to live with my grandparents.

Britain's Prime Minister Winston Churchill's aim was to gain overwhelming mastery of the air to demoralise the German population. The bomb attacks became more frequent over Berlin and Hamburg, my hometown, from March 1943. We had an eight-minute warning at school when the bombers approached and either had to run a thirty-minute walking distance home or try to find shelter on the way. I always ran home. In one instance I was shot at from a low-flying-small plane. I looked up, tripped on the kerb and fell. I stayed motionless. The plane flew off. The pilot probably thought he got me, but I thought *I tricked him!*

The now Air Chief Marshal Arthur Harris told his crew, 'you have the opportunity to burn out *the black heart* of the enemy', in Berlin.

In May 1943, the long African campaign ended with the allies taking control. Forty-one German submarines were sunk in three weeks. On 5 July, the battle of Kursk began.

In the same month British bombers (the Avro Lancaster) delivered 2,300 tons of bombs in the operation Gomorrah to Hamburg, followed by 8,000 pound 'blockbusters' and 4,000 pound 'cookie bombs', which knocked out roofs and windows, and subsequent waves of bombers dropped over 350,000 incendiary bombs to start fires. During that bombing, I was forgotten. By the time I reached it, the door of the bunker was closed. I watched the incendiary bombs in all colours. It looked like a Christmas tree. I was taken into the shelter a few minutes later.

Black smoke rose high in the sky. We couldn't see the sun for days. Fleeing people got stuck in the melting tar of the streets and were burnt with oil and phosphorus. The frustration of not being able to fight the fires was unbearable. There was no sand or running water. The water works were smashed first.

Most of our extended family was bombed out, but survived. My grandparents took three families into their big house, where they were safe for the rest of the war.

Ahead of the bombers allied planes spread strips of paper coated with aluminium foil on one side which blinded the German short-range radar. The code name for this action was *Window*. US bombers B-17 or *Flying fortress*es arrived the day after that bombing. Brigadier General Anderson Jr gave the order to target the Blohm & Voss Shipyards and Klöckner's aircraft engine factories. Stray bombs ended up in our district, though only one house was set on fire and the fire was extinguished in minutes. A part of a bomb landed in front of our kitchen window, but was quickly removed by the bomb squad. The house was not damaged. German fighters inflicted a heavy toll on American bombers. The bombers returned the next day but were blinded by smoke. This time it was a camouflage by German defence for certain sections of the city, but Blohm & Voss, the diesel engine works 'Man', the submarine bunkers on Finkenwerder and the power station were hit, leaving Hamburg without power for a fortnight.

In the raid on 27-28 July 1943, about 43,000 people were killed and over 16,000 residences destroyed. The defence in Hamburg increased by improving tactics with the flak, using Messerschmitt fighters flying over enemy bombers. But the bombing continued until the 2 August 1943. We were in and out of the bunker and running from the school. At one stage we nearly suffocated in the bunker because of gas coming through the air pump and the air pipe had to be closed.

In a mere ten days the residential areas and industry in Hamburg were reduced to rubble.

Here is a view of the firestorm from the suburbs of Hamburg.

This is what the Hamburg docks looked like after the raide. Cranes have collapsed and melted due to the intense heat.

Offenseive Tools of the Air War

The most famous of the RAF's heavy bombers, the Avro Lancaster entered service in 1942. It possesed a maximum speed of 280 mph and a range of 2,700 miles. A full load consisted of about 14,000 lbs. Protection consisted of ten .303 cal. machine guns.

Web Gallery

Designed for daylight bombing, the American B-17, or "Flying Fortress," had to be much more rugged and more heavily armed than its British counterparts which flew at night. Some B-17's carried as many as fifteen .50 cal. machine guns. These bombers were faster (at about 300 mph) than their British counterparts, but their load (6,000 lbs.) was much smaller. This B-17 could manage about 2,000 miles.

The Force-Wulfie FW-190 became Germany's leading interceptor in the later years of the war. Both this plane and the Messerschmitt were fairly small, fast and nimble.

This view depicts downtown Hamburg after the raid. The destruction is entirely characteristic of a firestorm. The walls of the buildings still stand, but everything whithin them has burned to cinders.

This is a view of the downtown area from the ground. Again once sees the empty shells of buildings. Note the rubble in the street from several of the structures that have collapsed.

The architect of this destruction was Air Chief Marshal Sir Arthur Harris ('Bomber' Harris). He had an unyielding hatred of Germany. His aim was to destroy Germany's cities.

As if the war was not enough, we had to combat children in the streets of our neighbourhood. Boys would not let us pass their street. They especially targeted my older sister, whom I defended fiercely. They finally gave up, because we used fists and fingernails and hit them wherever we could.

Sleeplessness and fear took hold of civilians, but it wasn't fear that preoccupied us. Our family was never afraid. All we thought of was survival. We were evacuated to Dresden. My father stayed home. He was a member of the SA (a kind of civil army). They formed the auxiliary kitchen and ran soup trucks on Sunday to feed needy people.

Although the bombing interrupted Hamburg's war industries, production recovered relatively quickly. By the end of 1943, the aircraft industry was operating at around ninety per cent of pre-bombing levels and electrical goods; optics and precision tools either returned or surpassed pre-bombing capacity. Most importantly, the submarine-building industry, which the allies targeted constantly, returned to pre-bombing capacity within two months. The bunkers were holding. By September, submarine WA 201 was completed and launched from Blohm & Voss, but the site was bombed again.

In September 1943, Italy surrendered to the allies.

In January 1944, Eisenhower became supreme commander of Western Allies' Forces.

The Allies concentrated bombers on Germany's fuel industry during day attacks.

On 6 June, American, British, and Canadian forces invaded France from the Normandy (D-Day). Germany attacked Britain with the first missile, the V-1, a few days later.

On 20 July, there was an assassination attempt on Hitler by a few of his officers, which he survived unharmed. He appointed a new chief of the army, General Guderian.

Russian troops marched towards Germany and the citizens of Warsaw started to revolt against German occupying forces. Germany attacked Britain with the first ballistic missile—the V-2.

Russia invaded Germany in January 1945 and liberated the Auschwitz death camp.

We were still in Dresden. Hearing the cannons at a distance, my mum organised a coach to take us to the station. The pram, hooked up at the back of the coach, was splashed with sludge from the melting snow. We took a train to Hamburg. A few days later the bombing of Dresden began.

Web Gallery

Another view of the damage from atop a church.

German civil defense officials collect bodies and start sifting through the rubble in the aftermath of the attack.

Web Gallery

The Cost: Desden (1945)

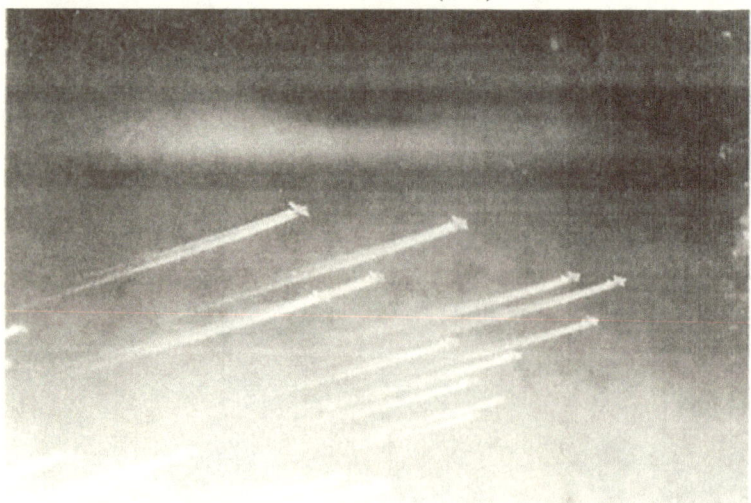

The View from Below: In the war's closing weeks, allied bombers launched as assault on Dresden, the crammed with refugees fleeing the Soviet army. The resulting firestorm devastated the city. No one has figured how many Germans perished in the attack, but estimates vary from 30,000 to 80,000. This is what B-17 bombers looked like from the groud in Dresden during the attack.

This is what downtown Dresden look like after the attack. Notice the similarities of Hamburg.

Overwhelmed by the scope of the attack, German officials could not bury the dead fast enough to prevent the outbreak of disease. They resorted to large pyres in an attempt to dispose of the great numbers of dead.

After arriving in Hamburg we found our house was still standing. My father was called up to the Russian front a few days later. We were devastated but before he went he gave me a book about the universe. We were watching the skies often and he explained the stars to me. It was the start of my fascination with the universe.

Shortly after that we had a strange experience. What was called a 'flying saucer' landed on one of the paddocks—near our house. We didn't go near it and heard later that the occupants (whatever they were) were killed by neighbours with dung forks. I was horrified. The 'saucer' was removed quickly. We never found out more about it.

Not much later, we had some news that a Jewish family related to us had left the country from Dresden, fled to Sweden and opened a chemist shop in Stockholm. Another aunt arrived from Dresden in Hamburg after being raped many times by the Russian soldiers. She died soon after.

I turned ten in February 1945 and was asked to join the Association of German Girls *(Bund Deutscher Mädel)*. My mother refused to send me and was threatened with being sent to a concentration camp. That was the first time we heard about them. But the war was all around us by then and they forgot about mum and me.

At one stage I travelled with my little brother to my grandparents by train. On route, our train came under attack. It was shot several times but not seriously damaged. It stopped at the next station. There was a large bunker in front of it, but the warden wouldn't let us in because it was full. So we had to run from tree to tree to the nearby hospital. We were taken in amongst the patients. The hospital was bombarded several times and we were shaken up while we were in the cellar. After the attack we could travel again.

In April, the front was on the opposite side of the river Elbe. We lived behind the hills and were fairly safe.

The allies liberated the Buchen and Dachau death camps. We heard about Mussolini's execution by the Italian resistance.

On 30 April 1945, Hitler committed suicide in his bunker in Berlin. Many Germans were in mourning. Germany's forces surrendered unconditionally on 8 May 1945. That was the end of the war in Europe. The remaining government was arrested and put on trial in Nuremberg.

My father was sent to Siberia as a prisoner of war. Our school was turned upside down by the English allies occupying Hamburg. The teachers were sacked and the books destroyed.

The battles continued in Japan. Russia had declared war on Japan. The US destroyed Hiroshima and Nagasaki with atomic bombs, which was the most horrendous experience of bombings and left shocking humanitarian after effects. Japan was defeated by the US on 14 August 1945 and surrendered on 2 September 1945, which finally ended World War II.

In June 1945, the victorious powers, the USA, Britain, Russia, and France assumed supreme authority. They wanted to curb Germany's appetite for conquest and destroy Prussia's stronghold on militarism, but they also wanted to keep Germany intact.

Germany was divided in four occupation zones. It was agreed that they should be preserved as an economic and political unit.

Germany was in ruins, but so were Britain, Japan, and other countries involved in this war. I am not blaming any country for what happened to Germany in World War II.

Hitler provoked the war, a war which caused immeasurable destruction and loss of human life in all these countries.

Our rations were severely restricted. We exchanged our rations for cigarettes and alcohol, for food and sugar. Meat was hardly available. We had to travel to other districts to get whale or horse meat or just blood (which we made into a sweet and sour dish with dumplings). We had to queue for everything. My mother went with an aunt and neighbours on overcrowded trains or boats to swap valuables for food.

The children helped the family get food by burrowing into the sheaves of wheat standing in stooks in the fields by cutting the heads of wheat inside of stook. We took the wheat seeds to the mill to exchange for flour. We went into the forests to collect mushrooms, blackberries, and blueberries. We grew lots of vegetables and fruits in our garden. Cooks from the Allied army kitchens came to exchange our vegies, especially our rhubarb, for chocolates, amongst other things. We became friends with them. We were remarkably healthy in spite of the shortages. There was certainly no obesity.

Our currency had hardly any value. My mother got eighty Reich's mark per month for the family of six. Our clothes were made of second-hand material or cloth. My mother was an excellent seamstress so we always looked decent. But in 1946, Germany started to receive foreign aid from America. The Marshall plan was to combat hunger, poverty, despair, and chaos with 1.4 billion dollars until 1952. This provided the crucial boost for the recovery.

We learned a lot from my mother during the war about skills of survival, to keep a timetable, and to be prepared and organised for all situations. We didn't receive any news from my father and didn't know if he was still alive.

My account about World War II is not meant to be complete. I have only written about events which were important to our lives.

In 1946, I sat for the test for high school behind my mother's back. My mother didn't want me to go to high school because we couldn't afford the things that were needed there like clothes, shoes, dancing and tennis lessons. All I wanted was to get an education for a better life. I was the only one of my primary school class to pass the test and win a scholarship not because of the best marks but because I had determination. My sisters and brother stayed in primary school until year nine.

THE POOREST CHILD IN THE RICHEST SCHOOL

- -

The closest high school (girl's school) was also the school for the richest girls. It wasn't easy to compete. Every time I was called up every girl looked around. When something was missing, I was accused of taking it. I was pushed, my pony tails pulled, and I was teased a lot because my father was a plumber and a mechanic (excellent in both trades). Their fathers were directors, bank managers, factory or business owners, or were working for the media.

As if that wasn't enough, my mother kept criticising me about my features—my long nose, big ears, unshaped lips, and likeness to my father's family, which she didn't like. I couldn't understand this because she put me together, but later I thought she must have been jealous because she wasn't allowed to have the education she wanted.

She also took my scholarship money. In spite of this she had such nice nicknames for me like 'owl' and 'absent professor'. I didn't mind that. The owl is the bird of wisdom and professors think a lot and I did.

To be able to take part in school excursions I started to do coaching for primary school and students from year five from the high school. I had usually two students.

After the basic subjects in year five and six such as German language, mathematics, biology, chemistry, physics, religion, gymnastics, volleyball, jumping, swimming, diving, and other competitive games, History, English, and Latin were introduced. I wasn't very interested in languages at that stage because I wanted to be a landscaper or economist, which would not require languages. The text of history books kept changing. I didn't trust any of that.

In those times undernourished students received cod liver oil and a meal a day at school to make up for the deficiencies in our diet. Needy families also received food parcels from the Quakers.

Then with my first English assignment, a story we had to recall by heart, something happened. I wrote down the whole story and after I finished I tried to compare it with the original under the desk. I got caught by my teacher. She marked my assignment with 'deception attempt'. I had no mistake in my assignment and didn't correct anything. I never forgot that experience, I was so embarrassed. I could hardly face school for some time, but I continued. It put a damper on my enthusiasm though, especially for that teacher. My results in English after that were only average. Fortunately, that teacher retired soon after.

It didn't take long before I had a problem with another teacher. I wrote a German assignment about 'a visit to a cinema'. I described every detail, from the pictures in front of the theatre, buying the tickets, entering the cinema, the voices, the cigarette smoke, the music and stage to the film. The teacher liked it and gave me high marks. I had to read it in front of the class. The girls protested and criticised it. I never got high marks again in spite of my great efforts.

I did enjoy sports and joined a sporting club. I entered competitions for running, relay races, javelin, shot put, jumping long and high, and gymnastics and gathered quite a few trophies.

In Latin we started with short stories and grammar and soon went to *Caesar de Bello Gallico*. While grammar was a good basis for Roman languages, *Caesar de Bello Gallico* was not very helpful for our lives.

In 1948, the economic situation in Germany started to change whith the currency reform from Reich's mark to deutsche mark. This was introduced to prevent stagnant capitalism and a centrally planned economy, which would have been a hindrance to creativity and initiative.

Savings of only sixty deutsche mark could be retained. Mortgages were reinstated and had to be paid again. Homeowners paid for their houses twice, including our family.

It didn't take long for me to become interested in politics. I joined the young socialists, where I met Anke, the daughter of our mayor. We became good friends and went on several international conferences in Belgium, Yugoslavia, and Germany together, where we met with other young socialists from all over Europe.

We both adored the opposition leader, Dr Kurt Schuhmacher, who was the bravest man I ever met. In World War I he was so badly wounded that his right arm had to be amputated. He returned to his studies in Berlin and graduated in law and politics. He became a dedicated democratic socialist. When the Nazi Party rose to prominence, Schumacher helped organise socialist militias to fight them. In 1930 he was elected to the national legislature—the Reichstag. At thirty-eight years old he was the youngest member of the Reichstag.

Because of the inability of the Social Democratic Party (SPD) and the Communist Party to form a united front, they couldn't prevent the Nazi uprising in 1933. Schumacher was arrested and spent the next ten years in different concentration camps. He risked his life through repeated defiance and hunger strikes. In 1943, when he was near his death, his brother-in-law succeeded in persuading the Nazis to release him into his custody. He was arrested again and was still in Neuengamme concentration camp when the British arrived and freed him.

He emerged an embittered man. He was in constant pain from his injuries. He was contemptuous, not only of the Nazis but towards everyone who didn't oppose them like he did. He reorganised the SPD and thought he was destined to lead Germany. He had enormous prestige, but the Americans didn't want socialism ruling Germany and were preparing Conrad Adenauer, a former mayor of Cologne, for leadership.

The new German politicians were discovered by the world and won respect by the allies. They also included Theodore Heuss, Ludwig Erhardt—the first Economics Minister (the locomotive of the economic miracle), Erich Ollenhauer, and the cosmopolitan Carlo Schmidt.

I followed politics closely. But let's come back to events in my school.

There was another change of teachers in year ten. A new head of the class taught mathematics. He was marked in the war by being trapped under the ruins of his house and had difficulty speaking. We also had a new teacher for German, history, and religion. The class was divided into two groups—mathematics and languages. I chose math. Our teacher was an amazing man. He made math so much fun that the girls in his class excelled in year twelve by covering the first semester of math and astronomy of the university. But I had problems with the teacher for German, history, and religion. He expected us to refer to the bible with every assignment in German. When he marked my assignment on 'The death penalty' less than average, I was so enraged that I showed it to the mayor, my friend's father. He was surprised about the mark and said it was an excellent argument.

I was determined to get justice and went to the headmistress of our school. She read the assignment and decided to mark my assignments after that. It still didn't make me feel comfortable at the school, but I persevered.

There was a great joy in our family when my father returned home after four years of imprisonment in Russia in 1949. I felt on that morning that that was the day when he would come home. I told my grandma (where my sisters and I stayed that day) about these feelings. She smacked my face for saying something like that, but I had telepathy with him while he was in Russia and I believe that may have kept him alive. I received the only card from him while he was in Russia, which didn't make me very popular with my mother.

My mother called with the news that he had returned. We went home and prepared a welcome while my parents were out to get him registered. When my parents entered the house we sang a homecoming song before we all stormed my father.

My father was in a terrible state of health but my mother soon revived him. He started to enjoy life again. A few months later, he found a job. He was a keen gardener and taught us how to grow things, to prune, to plan a garden and to store vegetables for the winter in barrows lined with straw. We all had a piece of the garden and could grow what we chose. We helped weed the big garden too. I loved it.

My mother started teaching all of us, four girls and my brother, cooking. We had competitions. Whoever could cook the tastiest and most economical meal received the highest points. The winner was given an award at the end of the competition. I won with blueberry pancakes. I picked the blueberries in the forest and had eggs from our chickens. I loved cooking. My mother could make a delicious meal with the most basic ingredients. She was a fabulously creative cook. I made my first cake when I was five years old. Mum was painting the girls' room. I wanted to help. She wouldn't let me paint but said I could make a cake. That was a great idea. I always watched her when she made cakes and started to make a sultana cake.

We also had to keep one room in the house clean for a week and were given points for our work. After a week we changed to another room.

Our family started to function again. The most peaceful picture was when my father sat down on Sunday mornings peeling potatoes (all the same shape), smoking a cigar, or whistling. He had a fabulous whistle. But there was a setback—my father didn't want me to continue my education. He said girls marry soon after school and don't need an education. Well, I continued high school and finished year twelve. In the end, he was kind of proud of me.

When I left school the teachers marked my subjects lower than my average marks but they did note that my composure was always very good, my attitude to my work during the whole time at school was commendable, as well as my never-tiring efforts to strive for my own genuine intellectual and spiritual achievements. I was glad to leave them behind.

My plans to be a landscaper would have taken an eight-year costly education. Through a friend of my mother I found a link to the public service. It was quite a challenge but I took it.

ADMINISTRATION IN THE GOVERNMENT OF HAMBURG

- -

T o be eligible for public service, we didn't only have to pass a test; we also had to prove that three generations of our family were without conviction. Twenty applicants out of four hundred were accepted, including ten females, the first time for the higher appointments to the public service. I was one of them.

On 1 April 1953, we were sworn in at a public ceremony in the town hall. I felt great. It was a new start. There were no great differences in our backgrounds and therefore no prejudice. I could be myself. We were enrolled in the Administrative College (which was exclusively for public service) for five years. The government paid for our education and a wage. I gave half of it to my mother.

The subjects in college turned out to be in the field of my interests— constitutional and state law, administration law, law science, personnel law, financial management, accounts, funds, economics, youth welfare, social welfare, taxation law. My interests were in law and economics.

The aim of our education was the preparation of the apprentice for administrative decisions and the formulation of administrative acts, developing a view on appeals, drafts of administrative guidelines, and technical instructions. To fill these requirements the apprentice had to be able to evaluate complicated matter, grasp the legal questions, apply relevant legislation and formulate a well-founded decision which stands up in court.

I met Marianne in college. We became good friends and competitors in class and together topped the class. This was a wonderful change after my experience in high school.

I commenced my employment at The Free and Hansestadt Hamburg as an administrative cadet on the Youth Board. I started training in the treasury, followed by the Department for Creativity and Culture, which included the Culture Ring for young people wanting to visit theatres at affordable prices (I was one of them). We had wonderful theatres, an opera house, and music hall in Hamburg in baroque style with lots of gold and royal red. I also worked in a home for difficult children and a District Juvenile Welfare Office.

During my first year of training, my father had a motorbike accident and suffered a double fractured scalp which left him constantly dizzy. By then I was transferred to a hospital where he was a patient. My mother, still jealous of me, did not want me to visit him. My father took his own life because he couldn't work anymore and felt useless. I was nearly sacked because of his suicide, which was seen as caused by mental illness. Mental illness in a family was not tolerated by the government.

We had to recite a story by Goethe's *The Journey to Rom* in front of the class in college at that time. I didn't read it because of the drama at home. I started to make it up when my teacher stopped me and asked if I had read it. I apologised but didn't tell him what happened. That was the only failure in my career. My mother had a breakdown and I looked after the family by budgeting, shopping, cooking, and sewing. We shared the cleaning.

I inherited valuable books from my father. They included *The Iliad* by Homer, a book about the universe and several volumes of the *Volkshochschule* (an adult education program).

On 1 April 1955, I was appointed Junior Assistant of the Higher Appointment Service and trained in the Taxation Department, Personnel Department of the Health Board, and the rates section of a council, where I received four marriage proposals. I celebrated my twenty-first birthday with twenty-one colleagues and I had to drink a cognac with every one of them. I was quite tipsy but walked home straight, without being detected by my mother.

But it wasn't only work. We had fun too, especially when I made unintended jokes. We celebrated birthdays, Christmas and even arranged a costume ball—Neptune and the mermaids. I dressed as a mermaid in a green dress, covered with black lace, fish earrings and a black veil with gold scales. There were fishing nets hanging from the ceiling and pots and other decorations from the sea. I didn't like dressing up, I'd rather go as myself, but it was good fun.

We had four weeks holidays and for special self-improvement another fortnight.

Marianne and I spent part of our holidays for eight years touring wine countries in Europe. We didn't drink much wine—only on occasions—but tasted hundreds and learned characteristics of varieties, regions, special vintages, and special vineyards. Our most memorable experience was in a cellar in Rhineland Pfalz, where the winemaker let us try one of his oldest red wines (sixty years old) on a tea spoon. We just nibbled on the thick wine but it gave us an experience beyond description of happiness, lightness, and a positive outlook into the world. I never forgot this experience.

Another part of my holidays was spent with one of my sisters on the island Sylt, where I loved swimming and baking in the sun and enjoying fresh shrimps when the boats came in. On a boat tour from the island to another island we were caught by a storm and were drenched on the way back to the boat. The captain treated us with gin and tea which was awful but saved us from the cold.

The special part of my holidays was dedicated to self-improvement. I chose painting. In my first course, I completed two crayon paintings of landscapes by working day and night. Others showed great appreciation for them. I donated them to the gallery in Hamburg and received a scroll of Athena, the goddess of wisdom and protector of owls, for them.

I finished my training and college in March 1958, with the examination for higher appointment service. We all passed the examination and were appointed Government Inspectors on 1 April 1958 in the town hall of Hamburg. A great celebration followed. Parents were invited. My mother did not attend. She thought I was selfish because I pursued my education. I didn't see it that way. It was what I wanted to do.

But my mother made me a wonderful *Baumkuchen*—a cake with lots of eggs, butter, almonds, apricot conserve, and rum. We celebrated at my grandparents' place.

I started on 1 April 1958 in a district juvenile welfare office where I acquired in-depth knowledge of youth welfare and family law in a short time. I was very lucky. For the selection of my jobs the government gave me positions where I didn't have to sit at the desk from nine to five.

Three cases during that period stick in my mind.

A baby girl was left by her mother, a prostitute, in a hospital. We found the grandparents in Eastern Germany. They lived in a small town near

Magdeburg. We confirmed that they were willing to take the baby. The question arose, who would take the baby to them? I volunteered. The baby was a lovely, very pretty little girl with brown eyes, dark hair, and olive skin. The Youth Board organised permission to travel into Eastern Germany and tickets for the train.

I felt very protective of that little baby. On the train, I was teased by other passengers for not wearing a ring. I smiled. Arriving at the destination I was checked out by authorities and received my points for food rations (I had long forgotten what that meant). I got twice the points as the citizens of the town.

Then I met the grandparents. They were so happy about our arrival and invited the whole neighbourhood to celebrate. The next day they organised the christening of the little girl and asked me to be the godmother. I accepted. It was a moving ceremony. The pig killed for a banquet was roasted on a spit and served with lots of vodka and goods out of their garden.

After the festivities I watched how they turned the offal of the pig into sausages and other smallgoods. It was a wonderful warm atmosphere; in spite of police watching every move. On the third day I was escorted by police to the station. Across the eastern border (the iron curtain) again, I was relieved to be back in the west.

The second case was quite dramatic. A man came into my office and wanted to kill me with a knife, because he didn't get custody of his child. The department manager heard the uproar and very calmly asked him into his office, where the man also calmed down when the decision was explained to him and upheld and I was rescued. I did breathe easier after he left.

In the third case, I received a message from the police that a baby was left in a tent on the river while the mother was working as a prostitute in town. I received an order from the court to remove the child. I left a copy of the order in the tent and took the crying baby by taxi to a home for orphans. I never heard from the mother.

After that I applied for a position in the law department of the Youth Board and was transferred. I worked with three men in the same room. There were phones ringing, discussions with clients, and a lot of smoke. The men were smoking constantly. I became an expert in the collection of maintenance, childcare fees and reimbursement, as well as deciding about custody disputes and social welfare issues. After a short time I was also involved in the preparations of social security and child protection legislation.

I enjoyed my work in the law department, but I had a great upset at home. My mother accused me of stealing money from her out of the drawer of her sewing machine, because I was sewing there. It was later found under her mattress, but I couldn't trust my mother anymore and moved in with my grandparents who had a free apartment on the top floor with a large balcony and view to the garden and surrounding area. This situation and my move did shake the family.

I looked after my grandfather, who had dementia from then on, besides working fulltime. I loved my grandfather. He was a quiet man, never upset, often sitting in the garden and thinking. I guessed he was very lonely. I bought my first car, a red VW with white interior, so I could come home faster from work.

One day, on the way home, I felt very weak and was just able to pull the car over to the kerb before I fainted. I went home after recovering and saw a doctor the next day.

The diagnosis was total exhaustion. I was sent on a holiday. When I returned, my grandfather had deteriorated and was sent to a hospital. He died soon after—alone!

While I was living in my grandparents' house I joined the Social Democratic Party (SPD) with its leader Helmut Schmidt. But to win the election Helmut Schmidt changed his policies and his character. I left the party because of that.

Soon after that, my grandmother decided to take her son and his wife into her home—into my apartment—and offered me one room. I talked about this to my dentist in the city (I always had bad teeth). He offered me his apartment joining the surgery. He had a house in a suburb. I was thrilled. It wasn't only near my office; it was also an icon of Hamburg-the *Chilehaus* (Chile House). I had a roof garden, a lift into my apartment, lots of high windows and central heating. It was perfect. I sold my car and was moved by my brother-in-law with his truck, which he normally used for produce for his business on markets.

Chilehaus

After settling in, I was looking for some fun. I joined a riding club and got myself a horse, a black temperamental stallion by the name of Boy. He stayed in the stable of the club where he was looked after by the master. We went riding out on the dykes along the river or into the marshlands and had breakfast with home-smoked (raw) bacon and cheese and homemade bread in their wonderful country home.

It didn't take long before there was a brutal interruption. In 1961, the Russians built a barrier along the eastern section and through Berlin, which was situated within the eastern sector. Berlin's ring traffic was cut in half and not functional any more. Transport was in chaos. West Germany's cities quickly organised buses for West Berlin to get the transport moving again. The union for the public service in Hamburg organised five buses. Because of the uncertainty and high risks for the lives of the participants when driving through the eastern sector to Berlin, the union asked for single people to travel in these buses to Berlin under the cover of a tourist group. I volunteered.

We were ready in a day and travelled from Hamburg to the eastern sector. When we arrived at the eastern border we were stopped and searched. We had no luggage and the officials were suspicious. Tanks accompanied us on both sides of the buses. We were stopped and searched over and over. We stayed calm.

Finally, we were allowed through Berlin's border. The reception of the Berliners was unforgettable. Berliners celebrated and invited us anywhere. Gradually, other buses arrived from other cities. All buses were handed over to Berlin's transport authorities.

We ended up in a lovely restaurant. The next day we were driven to the 'wall', which was topped with razor wire and loud speakers. The loud speakers were turned up to the limit. The sound of propaganda and watching the people from the east reaching through gates crying or calling for relatives was unbearable. I became violently ill. The bus had to stop. Another passenger got off behind me and was holding me. When I felt better I looked around and saw the most handsome man I had ever seen. We fell deeply in love that instant.

He was tall, had olive skin, deep blue eyes, and wavy grey hair. I felt utterly safe with him. We walked back to the bus hand in hand and stayed together talking the whole day. His name was Kurt. I learned he was the director of older people's homes, had been a pilot in the war and worked in the same building as me in the city. That was the good news, but then came the bad news—he was married. He told me about his wife and daughter. His wife was not interested in his career—only in food. She weighed over 120 kilo. He was not able to take her to presentations. I became very sad, but my love for him was so powerful I couldn't stop it. We danced the whole night and flew back to Hamburg on a chartered plane the next day.

Facing everyday problems at work and at home was not easy. The amazing thing was that the western allies voiced no opposition to the Berlin wall. Apart from some diplomatic protest, there was no action. The only agreement between east and west was the securing of free excess through the eastern sector and the guarantee of food supplies by airlift from President Kennedy.

Being home had a bright side—I could see Kurt every working day. We seemed to have telepathy. When we thought of each other, either of us would ring or we'd meet in the canteen and had a cup of coffee and a little chat. I bought myself a painting of two white swans as a symbol of our relationship, standing for grace, dignity and cleanliness. I did not believe that our love was wrong. It was so powerful that it seemed nothing could destroy it.

During this period, Chancellor Konrad Adenauer attached special importance to the restitution of Jews. He signed an agreement with Israel's Prime Minister Ben-Gurion for assistance for the integration of Jewish refugees in Israel with ninety billion marks. Six million Jews were killed in World War II. Jews are now living in Germany again. They own apartments, stores, play roles in the media, and have re-emerged in most communities.

Closer to home something else happened. France carried out an atomic test in the North Sea in 1962. This caused a ten-metre tsunami which flooded Holland and Hamburg. All of the flat country and houses in the inner city of Hamburg were flooded over the second floor. I lived on the fifth floor and was safe, but my sister rang after she fastened the roof window which blew out in the storm from the tsunami. She saved the roof by doing that—if not the house. My mother was with me that night. We couldn't go anywhere, the streets were under water.

The next day the water receded and I went to work. I asked for special leave because I wanted to volunteer in the rescue work. My boss didn't want me to go, but I explained to him that I couldn't work while people needed help urgently. He let me go. I was flown by helicopter to the island Finkenwerder, in the middle of the river Elbe. I was placed in a school on higher ground where I organised the rescue of older people and children who were flown to safety and from there sent into holiday homes. I also distributed food and clothing, which was flown in for people who stayed behind and the rescuers.

While I was busy doing this, Kurt came to check on me. He was on another mission. We were not in contact about this. I had no idea how he knew where I was. We both carried on with our work. When things seemed to be under control, I came down with a very high temperature (we worked day and night). Co-workers put me on a mattress and called an ambulance flight. I ended up in isolation in a hospital. They thought

I had typhus. I didn't trust my eyes when I had a visitor—Kurt. How did he know? I was released after they confirmed I was not contagious. Kurt took me home.

On the way we saw shop owners drying their stocks on the streets. Mail and receipts from the central post office were floating in the river Alster and lots of people were helping with the clean up. I reported back to work the next day but my boss wouldn't hear of this. He sent me on a holiday to a lovely resort. I missed Kurt.

Because our publishing company *Axel Springer* was flooded, no news about the tsunami got out of Hamburg. We handled the whole incident with the help of the army. My brother was in the team of the army which rescued the bodies from the river.

Things were running as normal soon afterwards.

I was appointed Special Employed Government Inspector for life in the town hall in 1962. I celebrated with Kurt. On that day I heard from a friend, who was retiring because of pregnancy, from the Health Board Department for Education. I was interested in education. I found it more and more difficult to work in the same building as Kurt because I wanted to be with him always, but didn't want to destroy the marriage. Our meetings were both joy and pain. Kurt could not imagine breaking his vows, because his wife was kind of helpless. So I took the opportunity and applied for my friend's job in the Health Board. My application was approved. I became manager of the Education Department in the Health Board, after I turned down the offer of the Youth Board to train me as a youth senator to keep me there.

In the Health Board I was also in charge of the higher instructions for hospital staff, testing of medical assistant personnel, hospital pharmacies, dispensaries, and handling pharmaceutical products in hospitals. This involved a lot of paperwork, which kept four secretaries busy. I was able to contribute to the tremendous improvement in the education of hospital personnel by coordinating all education plans of hospitals (nursing schools were in the hospitals, not universities) and planning a school for advanced education of all medical assistant personnel with programs and infrastructure. I introduced legislation for free education of technical assisting personnel, better conditions for dieticians, and more cooperation with professors from the university and lecturers in hospitals. This happened after I proved myself to them. At first I was only an inspector.

I made a speech in front of the head of the Health Board to point out the importance of diet in the healing process and the necessity to lift the status of dieticians. I received a standing ovation and a huge bunch of tulips. I was honoured. I thought I only did my duty.

Things like that happened frequently when I made special efforts to help people to get into the career they wanted to pursue but who didn't quite fill the requirements with their level of education. I arranged special tests or courses for them and ended up with cakes, flowers, and chocolates. We were not allowed to accept rewards for our work so I shared these things with my colleagues.

After a while I had to report to the senator of the Health Board direct. He used to call me into his office, a U-shaped room with a built-in aquarium around the wall. We would sit on swivel chairs and discuss new plans while watching the fish. He organised an official car for me, so I could move quickly from one appointment to another. It was all very challenging, but after a few months I was asked to take over the educational matters inside the system for the protection of civilians—starting a civil army.

I refused to do it. I was a peace worker and Gandhi follower. I didn't hate anyone, not even the pilot who shot at me. The director tried to give the portfolio to a colleague, because they didn't want to lose me but that was not successful because my colleague had no experience with education. So I got it back. I didn't want to get involved in the preparation for another war, but a public servant cannot refuse a job.

That's when I had my first thoughts of migrating. I didn't want to go alone and joined a marriage agency. In hindsight that was panicking. When I told Kurt about it we both cried for a long time. Our hearts were broken thinking of such a separation. I felt totally numb but promised myself that this was not the end. I would be back. I felt quite uneasy about my decision, but thought it was the right thing to do.

By that time my youngest sister was married and my oldest sister, with her husband and their first son, had migrated to Australia.

After a few failures in the marriage agency, I met Gabor, a very charming, good looking man and a new chapter in my life began. I finally ended paying supporting maintenance to my family, which I had done since I started work—even when I didn't live at home.

MARRIAGE TO A HUNGARIAN

Gabor hardly ever talked about his family or previous life. He was a refugee from Hungary, who had escaped from the Hungarian revolution to Austria and from there to Germany. He married an opera singer in Hamburg. She kept control over his money and fed him allegedly on potatoes in a jacket and cottage cheese. He told me he was a ballet dancer at that time and claimed she married him for his name. They were divorced. He also claimed he played eight instruments. He had a mandolin and a mouth organ. He had no money or assets.

When we met he worked in a company selling car parts. I felt sorry for him and felt ashamed that a German woman could treat him like that, but I didn't exactly fall in love with him. We found out soon that we had the same goals for the future, which included living on the land and raising a family. We searched the area surrounding Hamburg for land. It was hopeless because if there was land for sale it was out of reach of our budget. We found one very attractive block of ten acres, surrounded by scrub, but learned we wouldn't get a building license because it was near a sanctuary.

When I introduced him to my family, our relationship met with hostility. Gabor was not German. We were only to marry our own kind. I was a cosmopolitan and didn't think that that could be a problem. So we went our own way and the thought of migration grew. Our first intention was to join Albert Schweitzer in Africa. We admired his many ethical, theological, musical, medical, and administrative ideas and his selfless work in Africa for the sick and homeless, accompanied by his wife, Helen, who had a lot to offer him with her practicality and zeal. We wrote to him but never received an answer. Maybe we had no nursing experience, but we were prepared to do anything just to get involved in his wonderful work.

My dream was to be married by the time I was twenty-seven years old. I nearly made it. I had my tonsils out a week before the wedding and lost a lot of weight. My pretty white, shoulder-free satin wedding dress had to be altered. Gabor had a bit of a problem with the Catholic Church because he was divorced and I was Lutheran.

A day before our wedding, Kurt brought me an enormous bunch of sixty red carnations and assured me I would grow to love Gabor when we shared our lives together. That was the last time I saw Kurt. Gabor and I were married on 27 May 1963.

Our wedding was a big affair for family, neighbours, and friends. We drove to the Lutheran church, where friends and family had gathered, in a white coach drawn by white horses.

The Wedding

We were both very moved by the service and cried.

The reception was in our family home. Neighbours helped with the catering. We had over 200 guests, mainly my friends from the Youth and Health Boards. Gabor had three friends. He started to play the mandolin but it sounded awful. I stopped him and asked someone else to look after the music. It was a happy atmosphere. We were given many hugs and presents. After a walk through the garden, music played again and there was dancing, champagne, wine, and liqueurs. Visitors were coming and going for hours.

We took off in the afternoon and went to my apartment. We told everybody we were going on a secret honeymoon, but stayed in my apartment. The wedding night was a great disappointment. After making love once Gabor said we had to restrict ourselves with sex and went into the second bedroom. I had no idea why he left me. It killed all my feelings for him. I thought when you are married you make love when you feel like it. We still made the best of our 'honeymoon' with outings to parks and rivers.

Years later, Gabor told me he had a dream that the Pope (John XXIII, who died ten days later) gave us his blessing which made him drawn back to the Catholic Church. He explained to me that Catholics were supposed to control their sex life. I wanted children.

That was the first difference in our upbringing. Apart from that it didn't have a big influence on our lives because neither of us went to church very often. But then other problems emerged. Gabor was the last of nine children in the family. When he was born his mother bathed him and put him to sleep and then had to go out into the fields again and help his father. This is the way many country men treat their women in Hungary. I was a city girl and was respected in Germany. I now know that it is very important when someone marries a person from another culture to make sure they are compatible, otherwise it can lead to great disappointments, misunderstandings, and frustration.

After waiting for about two months, we approached the Australian Embassy for an immigration permit because my sister lived there and we thought it was the most peaceful country. We had not heard that Australia was involved in so many wars, because Australian forces never occupied land afterwards.

Then we informed our employers about our plans. I was offered an immediate promotion with the endorsement that I accomplished more than ten other officers would have done in the same time. Gabor got an offer from Opel for a position as manager of their spare part division. Neither of us accepted the offers.

It took six months for us to be accepted as migrants to Australia. I was the problem because I worked with secrets and I raised suspicion because I was leaving the public service, which was unheard of. Finally, we received the boarding papers for the Italian passenger ship *Aurelia,* which sailed in December 1963. My family was so angry they didn't even send us off.

MIGRATION TO AUSTRALIA

We were sharing a cabin with another couple and slept on a double bunk. The first stop was Southampton to take more migrants on board. From there we sailed right into a violent storm, which started while we were sailing through the strait of Gibraltar into the Mediterranean Sea. Plates were skidding off the tables, people became seasick, and we had to be tied to our beds. We could hardly eat.

By the time we got to Port Said the storm had calmed. We joined a bus trip to Cairo which was a stunning experience. We were confronted by a huge city with a history and culture dating back to thousands of years. I was especially impressed by the mosques, which were made from alabaster and decorated with precious stones. The architecture was equally striking.

We admired the treasures in the museum, where we saw mummies of rulers in golden cases, golden ornaments with inlaid gems, jewellery, and an incredible display of weapons, which were gathered in the Pyramids of Giza on the south western fringe of Cairo. The colourful market, which only opened at night, was a fairy land with the lights, the reflections in the jewellery, giftware, and souvenirs. The music and of course the bartering and haggling added to the atmosphere. It was great fun and an unforgettable experience.

We stayed in a hotel and went on a camel ride to the pyramids the next day. Getting on to a camel was quite an adventure and the ride was like being on a boat on choppy waters. The sight of the pyramids was like being transferred back through the millennia. We wondered how they could have moved the colossal stone blocks without any cranes. Climbing into them was not easy. The passageways were narrow tunnels but there was nothing at the end. The pyramids were empty. A lot of treasures had been robbed or taken by explorers. Some treasures ended up in Cairo and other museums.

From Cairo we went by bus through streets fenced with razor wire and guarded by the military. We passed cemeteries for pets and people. Graves for the pets, especially cats, were much more ostentatious than for people. We drove through very poor villages until we finally reached Suez.

Suez is one of Egypt's largest ports and is situated near the scenic Ataga Hills. It has an excellent view of Sinai and the Red Sea. Since the opening of the Canal Suez has grown into a prosperous modern city—the best place we saw in Egypt.

After a city tour we returned to catch our ship, an adventure in itself. We had to jump from a small boat onto a lowered bridge of the ship while the boat and the ship were both speeding in nearly dark conditions. On board the ship we sighed with relief and were happy that we made it.

We were sailing smoothly to our next stop—Aden in Yemen. We received a warm welcome from traders in their colourful boats loaded with souvenirs, jewellery, handicrafts, and varied headgears. It was a hustle and bustle with wheeler-dealers trying to make quick business. It was good fun until we went ashore.

Aden was the worst experience we had on our trip. People were so poor they lived in cardboard huts or just a rug on the footpath. Beggars were everywhere. Butchers had their meat hanging outside, covered with flies! There was also a 'market' under a tent, where fruit and clothes were sold. Dust was everywhere. We were glad to board the ship again.

Through the Gulf of Aden we sailed into the Indian Ocean. Our passenger list increased, by lots of flying fish. Dolphins kept us company for long stretches. The water was so clear we could watch the spectacular life of the ocean.

While we were enjoying this, we started talking to other passengers about expectations of Australia and the English language (I knew only Shakespeare English, which turned out not to be very practical). Gabor knew hardly any English, so we participated in English lessons on board. We also discussed job opportunities and other destinations for migrants. Some people were going to New Zealand and called it the best place in the world. Others talked about Queensland, especially Cairns, and described it in beautiful colours. We were heading for Adelaide to meet my sister. After weeks on the water the first sight of land in the sunrise was quite unexpected. The excitement was overwhelming. Our new world was awaiting us. What would it be like?

We anchored in Fremantle and had a chance to tour Perth by bus. We stayed in Fremantle. The people were so friendly, showing us the town with its lovely buildings, shops, and the colourful splendour of the gardens. The streets were lined with hibiscus, oleander, and roses. They told us about jobs and places to live and tried to convince us to stay. It was very tempting. We later wished we had, but we were to meet my sister and our luggage was going to Adelaide. We found it very hard to part from these lovely people.

Two days later we disembarked in Melbourne. It was such a change from Fremantle. The city reminded me of Hamburg—all grey. We stayed only one day then boarded a train to Adelaide. We travelled through unfamiliar countryside, but it looked very challenging. We were dreaming of a farm.

Then came the great moment . . . Adelaide terminal! It didn't look like a terminal, more like a station in a suburb, but there was my sister, accompanied by a friend.

I hadn't seen my sister in ten years, but she hadn't changed. Our welcome wasn't as warm as I imagined it would be. I had the feeling that she was preoccupied. Nevertheless, I was so grateful that she saved us from going into the migration camp in Bonegilla in Victoria.

We went from the station to the Central Market, the only place for continental small goods. There wasn't a good choice, but there was a great range of fruit and vegetables we had never seen before. We looked forward to trying a lot of these new foods. After our little shopping spree we were taken to my sister's dairy farm at Yankalilla, south of Adelaide. Here we met my brother-in-law and their now three sons and learned the cause of my sister's reserved greeting. My brother-in-law had just had an accident and wasn't able to work. Money was tight.

My husband and my brother-in-law didn't see eye to eye. If a visiting friend of the family hadn't turned up a few days later they would have probably killed each other. The friend took us to Adelaide where he knew of a vacant place near his home. He introduced us to the owner of the place. It was a small red brick house with one bedroom and a lounge. We rented the house and bought a lounge suite the next day. The couch could be converted into a double bed.

A few days later that friend came back and found Gabor a job in the company where he worked. Gabor had to start in a foundry, which was tough.

We looked around for a house and found a builder who showed us his developments.

We didn't like the area with houses for sale, but then he mentioned he was building houses in 'Paradise'! We liked the sound of that and studied the plans for that area. There was a roomy three bedroom cream brick house with large windows near the reservoir and the hills in a lovely landscape. It looked like 'Paradise' to us. It felt right. The lump sum I got for my service with the government and my savings were a good deposit for the house.

The shell of the house was already standing. We sat down with the builder and discussed the colour scheme for the inside walls and tiles and all the fittings in bathroom and kitchen. We had to use body language to aid our limited English.

I decided then that my next step would be to learn everyday English since every new area we came across had a language of its own. I also needed to find a job. Through migration officials, I found a teacher who taught correspondence courses. I enrolled and found this was a very good way to learn the words I needed for the house and shopping.

Finding a job was a different matter. I learned my education would not be accepted because Australia had no education equal to mine. I had to do new studies in Australia or accept any job available. I didn't want to lose much time or savings (which were meant for a deposit on the house) and decided on the latter, because our goal was to live on a farm. But we had to get to know the country first.

The house was ready in three months. We moved in on 27 May (our wedding day) in 1964. We felt very proud—our first house! We would have never achieved that in Germany.

After buying some more furniture, I got a tip from a neighbour that there were cleaner jobs available at the university. I made some inquiries and gained a job as a cleaner for a lecture room and some offices. We had a shift of four hours from six to ten in the morning, three hours' work and one hour break. I met the other cleaners during the break and became friendly with a Scottish lady who was a librarian in Scotland. She was teaching me English during the break by pointing out everything around me and telling me the English word for it. I picked up her Scottish accent without noticing it.

While I was working there I had my first miscarriage. I was heartbroken after being overjoyed to be pregnant.

Three months later, I applied for a job as a shop assistant at a new supermarket.

I was employed as the dairy and frozen food manageress and had to organise the display for the opening. It was quite a challenge, but I had a good knowledge of continental food and storage and handling of food. The opening was a celebration. We had extra specials like butter for half price. People poured in. Butter was the favourite. I carried dozens and dozens of boxes into the shop. I enjoyed it very much, especially because I had a very understanding manager when I misunderstood something or didn't know a grocery line when I was questioned by customers. I always tried to find out about it. He made it easy for me to become familiar with my stock and when ordering produce. We had quite a few laughs when I was not aware of the double meaning of some words like 'sponge' for cake and a cleaning sponge. At one stage the manager asked me when we were sorting frozen turkeys to bring one from the counter. I thought there is no turkey on the counter—thinking of the checkout— and brought him a checkout girl. He said that is not a turkey! Everybody laughed. I had no idea that he called the freezer a 'counter'. I learned quickly. With my English improving, the work became easier.

We only lived in Paradise for one year. It wasn't Paradise—only the garden, it would grow anything we wanted. Our house was built on deep black 'Bay of Biscay' soil, which was moving with every different moisture level, causing cracks in the house, in spite of the house being built on a special foundation. I filled the cracks weekly. We were very disappointed, but it spurred us on to look for a farm.

We met a German real estate agent who took us into the wine-growing country in McLaren Flat, south of Adelaide. We found two places in the area with a few acres of established, but neglected vines. One place on a hillside had a house on it and also some apricot and almond trees. Thirty beehives were also included. Both places had undeveloped areas. We signed a contract for both blocks and put our house on the market. The house was sold within our cooling-off period and we had the deposit for the two blocks.

Then we had another problem to solve. We had no transport. That was no problem in the city, where there was plenty of public transport, but in the country we needed a car. Our neighbour in Paradise, a young Italian, came to our rescue. He found us an old sturdy Vanguard in driving condition. That was not the end of the problem, as neither of us had an Australian driver's license. The neighbour offered to look after the car until we had a chance to pick it up.

We arranged a removalist and were able to travel with him. Our move happened to be again on our wedding day, 27 May 1965. After all the packing, the drive through beautiful countryside was a wonderfully relaxing experience. We were driving towards the fulfilment of our dream!

LIVING ON THE LAND

My love for the land and nature started to grow in our garden and on one of my aunt's farms in a suburb of Hamburg and was increased by outings into the countryside with the family. Ancestors on my father's side were big landowners in Denmark and Germany. My father's father sold his farm to live in the city. He was an alcoholic and lazy. Now we had a farm!

We moved on a beautiful autumn day. We had to swap our beautiful St Ann's bedroom suite for a smaller one with the new owners of our house because their suite was much smaller than ours and fitted into our two-bedroom farmhouse.

Our boxes could wait. We wanted to have a good look at the place and walked to the top of the hill. We had the most wonderful view over the whole valley. We learned later that our sand hill was part of a forty-thousand-year-old sand dune. It was our first established vineyard of non-irrigated Grenache vines. We just sat there taking it all in.

Our farm one year later

Taken the next year!

Our place was much neglected. It was previously owned by a widow with six children. Looking all over it we saw the potential and started to make plans.

First, we needed to do some clearing of the undeveloped land which was ferny and swampy. There would be further vineyards and a market garden in between while the vines were small. We would also have to buy a tractor and a ripper.

Returning home we felt full of purpose and very happy. Our home offered another challenge. Our kitchen had a woodstove and a small electric stove. The laundry was equipped with a trough and washboard. What a change to the service I had in Hamburg. My washing was picked up and delivered back ironed and mended, if necessary. Here we go. I was learning. I loved the woodstove and made bread in it. The cooking was much tastier. But the laundry was another matter.

We found a second-hand tractor and a ripper and had a present from a friend of my sister's family—a disc plough. This was perfect for the start. The clearing began. I soon had to revise my romantic ideas about 'living on the land' and learn how to live off the land. After clearing the first two acres we planted potatoes. They were caught by two nights of frost. Our place was supposed to be in a frost-free area.

After three months we were both working fulltime again. Gabor had a job in the meatworks and later at Chrysler in another foundry (we always had to take the hardest jobs) and I worked for a new supermarket—only at half the distance as the previous store—with the same manager I had in the first store. Our money went to pay off the mortgage and a deposit on a new tractor. Our first tractor had given up the ghost with all the clearing. We lived from our products and swapped with honey, wine, and vegetables for fish and clothes.

We started to have pets, a lovely, white, Persian cat and chickens. It worked out fabulously. But then things started to go wrong. I had an ectopic pregnancy and the doctor ordered strict bed rest. My husband was not impressed. By his upbringing a woman is not a woman when she can't have children. I was pregnant for four months and the tube burst. I was alone at home, Gabor was in the city. I was in excruciating pain. I got out of bed and tried to ring the doctor. I fainted on the way to the phone and was out for a while. When I regained consciousness, I rang my next door neighbour. He came straight away and called my doctor who rang the ambulance. I was carried on a sheet into the car and was then taken to Adelaide.

It was a long trip. I lost a lot of blood. In the hospital I was attended to straight away and put on a drip. I was operated on in a very short time and received a large volume of blood and serum in a transfusion.

During the operation I had an out-of-body experience. I was a small cloud next to an enormous cloud which was spreading something.

I asked, 'what are you spreading there?' and was given the answer, 'the good and the bad chances on earth'. I was curious. 'Why are you spreading the good chances there and the bad ones here?' The answer came, 'if I do it the other way around, I'll get the same question.' That meant to me, I had to cope with whatever befell me.

When I woke, after the anaesthetic wore off, a sister was sitting on my bedside and asked me to get up. I said I couldn't. I was again in excruciating pain. She said, 'yes you can'. I answered 'no' twice more and she repeated 'yes' every time. Not believing her, I tried. I did walk a few steps to the window but became very dizzy. The sister said, 'you must have milk!' And so it was. She led me back to bed and gave me a pump. They saved the milk for another baby. I cried.

When I was released I didn't feel well at all. I thought something was wrong with my blood. I had unusual ideas. The experience that I thought I could not get up, but could when I tried made me think I'd like to start a hospital and encourage people like the sister did with me. You can if you try! My idea was strongly opposed by my husband and friends. I resigned to stay quiet and resumed my duties on the farm after my husband told me that I only went into hospital to escape work on the farm. This is an attitude of some Hungarian farmers, though probably not all of them. I wrote a letter to Kurt after that. It was returned from the personnel office with a letter of regret. Kurt had died from cancer. He was the healthiest man I knew when I left him. I was devastated. I was totally hopeless.

During my work at the supermarket my manager was invited to a wine-tasting by Tolley's winery in our shopping centre. He gave me the invitation because he knew I had a history with wine-tasting and would appreciate it. I went and was introduced to a number of wines without making a comment. Then the representative asked me what I thought about them. To be quite honest, I wasn't that impressed and gave the analysis of what was wrong with the wines such as too long left on the skins, hot fermentation, stalks not fully removed, maturing time in oak, and more. They were intrigued and invited me to their Tasting Board. I felt very honoured and tempted because I received more recognition from them than from my husband, but by then we had plans for our own winery.

Soon after that we went to the stock market to buy a pig, which we could feed with the vegetable waste. We thought we had bid for one only but realised at the end of the auction we had bought the whole lot of the yard (eight). Well, we had to build a yard and pigsty to accommodate them. We had to put them in the chicken coop first. The next day Gabor went out to get the timber for the pigsty and I was weeding the potatoes in the front yard. Suddenly I heard an explosion, I looked around and saw smoke coming out of both sides of our house. I ran back, grabbed the hose, but was too shaky to fit it to the tap.

A neighbour came to my rescue and put the fire out before the fire brigade arrived.

The fire started in our spare room where I had placed the newly-arrived chickens in a cardboard box (packaging from our lawn mower) with a light globe to warm them. The fire burnt out that room with almost all my books (over 500) except the bible, Gandhi's life story, my book about the universe and several books of philosophy. Our slides and the glory box with all the wedding presents were also lost. The rest of the house was badly smoke-damaged. One of the chickens survived behind the built-in kitchen cupboard. We had no idea how it could have got there.

One of the farmers we helped with the harvest lent us his caravan. We could still use the bathroom.

We contacted the insurance company. They sent us a builder for a quote for the repair and repainting of the house. It was over £4,000.

Our insurance was £2,000, which was paid by the company. We made a deal with the builder (who later bought a vineyard because he came to love the area) to look after his vineyard for two years and pay the balance with this and other contract work. We were grateful for this solution but it was hard work beside all our other jobs for two years. We had to meet our commitments for the new tractor as well, but we couldn't make any further payments on our second block. We lost the block and the deposit of £1,000.

We used the insurance money for the contents to buy a Volkswagen van to be able to transport our produce to the markets. Until then the greengrocer of the adjacent town took our produce when he went to the market, but refused to do it after we bought our new tractor.

We were able to sell our potatoes to the Potato Board and they helped us with waste potatoes for the pigs. The wholesaler of the main market gave us $2,000 (we had a currency change during that time) without a contract, interests or security, just to be paid back when we could afford it. Neighbours helped with donations and the most important thing . . . a washing machine. It all showed us how wonderful Australian people are!

A few months after the house fire, my mother came to visit us. She was quite distraught about the way we lived and how Gabor treated me. She wanted to take me home with her. But I was married and wanted to keep my vows. I still saw a good future for us.

Through contract pruning we acquired cuttings from the famous Hardy winery and planted our newly cleared acres with Grenache and Shiraz. In between the rows we had radishes (three times a season), spring onions, tomatoes, sweet corn, and beans. Cucumbers grew very well in the swamp area without irrigation. Everything had to grow without fertiliser, because we had no money for it, but it did. It was virgin soil.

We collected fowl manure from a layer shed which contained lots of eggs (a protein enrichment for the ground) in the neighbourhood for the established vineyard. I spread the manure while Gabor was at work. Because of the heavy load the tractor's front came up at one stage and was swinging from one side to the other. I didn't know what to do. Finally, I got it down again with the brakes and unloaded some of the manure.

We had a tremendous crop the next year. The contractor who delivered our grapes to a winery said he had never seen a crop like that from our block. After that we used our grapes to make our own wine from the 1968 vintage on. We stored it in our back veranda and the next year in the garage.

We had no equipment. The first investment was a mangle (with the addition of a funnel) and a bath tub for the crushing. We bought a number of barrels, puncheons and a fermentation barrel. After paying for all the barrels I had $200 left, which I took to a solicitor and asked him to get us a winery license to enable us to sell the wine. He thought I was completely out of my mind and said that we would never get a winery. I replied, 'you watch', and insisted on my request. We paid his fees off with our wages.

The winery was designed by Gabor but had to be approved by an architect. The architect was an arrogant man. He had to endure a bite from our dog when he put his hand in the car where the dog was kept when we had visitors.

Before we started building the winery we decided we wanted to adopt a baby. I had had four miscarriages and had no hope of carrying a baby. Tension in our marriage was building because of my failure to have a baby. I was hoping an adoption would fill the gap. We applied for the adoption of a boy.

ADOPTION OF MY SON

We had two discussions with the Adoption Centre and a visit from an officer from there and were given approval for an adoption. We were told the waiting time would be around two years.

We were totally taken by surprise when we received a call a fortnight later that our baby had arrived in the Mother and Children's Hospital. Gabor was asleep after his night shift, but I woke him screaming, 'our baby has arrived!' We didn't have anything prepared—clothing, bedding, pram, or anything. We just jumped into the car and made a shopping list on the way to the city. We bought everything we thought we needed in our favourite department store and loaded the car. Then it was off to the hospital.

We were told by the Adoption Centre that the baby's natural mother was a pianist and the father a mariner, which we later discovered was totally untrue. The mother was a checkout operator in a supermarket and the father was an alcoholic when Robbie found him in later years.

We were so excited. We had no idea what to expect when we were welcomed by the leading sister of the hospital. She took us to the nursery. Another sister went to fetch 'our little boy'. She met us with this tiny bundle (he was 6.5 pounds) in her arms and put him in mine. I looked into his red little face with blue eyes and dark hair and he smiled at me. He was two weeks old! I was so touched and happy. When the sister asked, 'would you like to take him home?' I thought, *who could say no to that? He needs me!*

She showed us how to handle him and what to feed him. Gabor didn't say much. I was wondering what he thought. Of course we took him home. On the way we went to the chemist and bought his formula and a few other things for our brand new baby and showed him off to the chemist. He said, 'you've got yourself an Indian!' because he was so red.

We named him Robert and called him Robbie.

In spite of the fact, that I looked after my brother, when I was very young, I felt quite anxious that I did everything right. My mother was there when I looked after my brother, but she was in Germany, not here. A very friendly neighbour from next door took her place and gave me advice whenever I needed it.

It was a very hot summer. We had no air conditioning and we had to keep him cool. I spread a wet sheet over his cot and dressed him only in cloth nappies.

He had a very strong mind and knew exactly what he wanted and protested when I didn't know it. I kept a regular timetable and he was very good. He slept through the night within weeks. He was a very serious child and reminded me of my father. I took him in the pram whenever I worked on the farm. When that was on the hill, I put the pram on a tray of the tractor so I could always communicate with him. Gabor was sometimes envious of the attention I gave Robbie and called me away to do some work for him. We had to prove for three months that we could look after Robbie properly before we could apply for the legal adoption at the court. It all went well and we celebrated.

Then the next big event had to be tackled—building the winery.

THE WINERY

The origins of winemaking in the Hungarian style can be traced back to the sixteenth century in Gabor's family on their properties in Bacska-Banat. After the First World War, the extensive vineyards of the family fell into Yugoslavian hands.

Gabor's father settled after that in Szeged (Hungary), where he later established his own vineyard and managed another estate. Gabor took a great interest in his father's work and learnt by the time he left Hungary in 1947 all his father's traditional techniques to carry on his wine making, which was done in accordance with the principles of organic farming. Organic farming in Hungary then strictly excluded the use of artificial chemical fertilisers, pesticides, fungicides, and herbicides. Only organic animal and green manure like lupins, broad beans, and peas were used in the vineyard. The wine was made without sulphur or other additives like colour and flavour.

The definition of organic wine varies today in different countries. Wine without sulphur is consumed for its health benefits.

After studying modern techniques of wine making, Gabor decided there was no need to interfere with nature adding colour, flavour, yeast, and chemicals to the wine. Using healthy late-picked grapes, which produce rich flavours, rich colour, and high alcohol content guarantees long-keeping qualities. Slow fermentation and long maturing in oak gives the wine a special character. The wine improves with aging as flavours become more integrated and balanced.

Our organic methods and the resulting quality of our wine got us the production license for the winery in November 1969. Gabor was the wine maker, doing the technical work and planning with his engineer brains. I shared the enthusiasm for organic wines the *Hungarian style* with Gabor. Because of my knowledge in economics, law, accountancy, taxation, and administration, and of course my experience of wine tasting, I was able to handle the management of the winery and the sales of the wine. It seemed to be a perfect partnership.

The work on the building was soon to begin. We found some big iron telephone posts on the dump and decided they could be the main support for the construction.

Gabor did all the measurements and I helped with placing the posts in position. At one stage, our German shepherd dog decided he wanted to play and put sticks in the postholes where we were working. I tried to take him to his place to chain him up, but he had other ideas. He growled at me in the voice of a wolf, jumped up on me, and bit me all over my body. Gabor, disturbed by the noise, grabbed him, tied him up, and shot him.

I was black all over. We were very upset. The dog was always growling when he didn't like something. I didn't trust him. He must have felt that. We buried him under a tree and continued work the next day.

When all the posts were in place we bought the timber for the frame work. Gabor was the builder and I was the handyman—handing up tools, nails, and holding things in place.

One day, I called Gabor for lunch and when he didn't turn up after a while, I checked what was happening and found him on the ground under the construction. He was hurt and in pain. A check-up at the doctor showed he had a broken collarbone and they couldn't do a thing about it. Gabor continued with the construction in spite of it.

Before we finished the building we had a bushfire, coming from the other side of our hill. It looked pretty scary. Gabor went much closer to the fire with the tractor and ploughed a break. I was watching with my neighbour, holding Robbie in my arms.

I was always afraid of fires, but Gabor saved our vineyard and most likely the property. He came back looking like a chimney cleaner from all the smoke.

We continued our construction work the next day. Robbie was always our companion, first in the pram, then in a pen with his own plastic tools. He tried to cut the framework at one stage with his little saw and really put a dent in it.

We finished the building alone. The only help we had was the reinforced concrete floor.

When the panelling in the tasting area was done and the carpet lay
down, we put in a desk, which we also used as a counter. We created a
half-barrel shaped display for our wines. We installed the art of many
local artists with paintings, pottery and china paintings to the tasting
area. We found a very talented Italian printer who designed and printed
our labels. These really made an impression.

After shifting the barrels into the winery with a forklift on the tractor, the bottling began. We used natural corks and dipped the top of the bottles in red coloured wax so they could breathe—no caps.

It was fascinating to discover the connections in the industry—mainly suppliers. We didn't know anybody but we soon made many friends in the business. We applied for and received a 'cellar door' license in 1972. We had the first tasting room in the district. I typed a letter of invitation to our friends and acquaintances for the opening of our cellar door. We had an excellent response. I started a card file for people I connected with to be added to the list of our friends and kept a record of our visitors in a visitor's book.

The word spread by mouth, we did not have any advertising. The media became interested. Brian Chatterton wrote the first article about our wines under *Sunday Mail Winery Guide* in December 1972. He called our wines some of the most unusual wines he had tasted and described our different way of wine making. He was surprised that we made our red and white wine, McLaren Ruby and McLaren Gold, mainly from late-picked grenache. For the white wine we removed the juice immediately from the skin. The wine had a rich golden colour.

He asked the public to judge the wines with a completely open mind and not to compare them with other wines. We had natural wines without any additives, they had to be different. At that stage we were the only winery in Australia to make natural wines. People who could not tolerate commercial wines could drink our wines without the side effects of headaches, asthma, and sinus trouble because our wines did not contain sulphur dioxide. Customers streamed in from all over Australia but there were very few locals. Our wines were sold out for two years ahead!

Robbie was christened in the Lutheran Church that year.

We were busy but we were also thinking of completing our family and applied for the adoption of a girl. We were again very successful and our beautiful girl, who we named Tamara, arrived at the end of the year. Tamara had olive skin, dark brown eyes, and dark hair. She had some resemblance to Gabor.

For one reason or another, tension grew between Gabor and me. Tamara must have sensed that. Just before we were able to adopt her legally, after three months she was very difficult to feed and developed asthma. It was so bad she had to be admitted to a hospital and was put into a tent. I felt so helpless. Gabor didn't want to take her back.

He made it clear to the adoption centre that he only wanted a healthy child. I was heartbroken. She was my child by then. I loved her dearly, so did Robbie. I could not be comforted for a long time. My doctor found another nice family for her and he kept me informed about her development.

Robbie was always with us until he started kindergarten. He was spoiled by the customers but he entertained them with his music box and playing a guitar like Elvis Presley.

As if the involvement with the winery was not enough, Gabor made the heroic effort to dig a trench through our two acre swamp with a spade (we could not afford any machinery at that stage) to drain the area into our well in the centre of the property.

Brian Chatterton published another article in the *Sunday Mail Winery Guide* in 1972. I handled the media at the beginning because Gabor's English was still not very fluent. Gabor seemed to resent that.

In that year we had the first Bushing festival. I was holding a wine tasting in the festival town McLaren Vale-with Robbie in the pram while Gabor entertained visitors in the winery.

Before the dinner party I met the Premier Don Dustan who had just returned from my home town, Hamburg. We started talking about Hamburg, his experience with the people there, went on to his cooking book, then his garden and we didn't notice that everyone was waiting for the premier to open the festival. I was not very popular. But Don Dunstan and I became lifelong friends.

The premier had something else to celebrate that year—the opening of the Adelaide Festival Theatre, which we unfortunately could not attend because we were too busy in the winery. I received a wonderful recording from him on which he recites *Desiderata* and speaks about his son on side two.

Our winery was the only one to get attention from the *Women's weekly* at the Bushing Festival. This caused some envious remarks from the commercial wineries.

The article stated that we had experienced instant success and had three vintages sold out already—a double cause for celebration. Yes, we did celebrate! And we had lots of visitors.

Amongst all this hustle and bustle, an opportunity opened for me when our neighbour's son wanted to sell his V8 Valiant. It looked very smart in its blue and white finish. I wanted it for myself since Gabor bought the Volkswagen in his name (we had everything else in joint names). I bought it. I had to take a driver's test. Gabor was my driving instructor (don't let your husband teach you to drive!). I passed the test with no problems, not just because our policeman was a regular customer.

We took the car on our first holiday to the Coorong. Gabor was driving most of the way because I had a migraine (which was not unusual). On the way we visited a farm, which had peacocks and guinea fowl advertised. We bought two peacocks and six guinea fowls and put them in the cage, which we brought along. No hotel wanted us with that cargo, but finally we found a motel and kept our passengers a secret.

It was a wonderful week. On the way back, we stopped at SAFCOL's fish factory and stocked up with delicious frozen crayfish meat.

My friend and neighbour, Betty, was managing the winery in our absence. She did a wonderful job. After that we did arrange breaks for swimming and walking on the nearby beach. I can still hear Robbie calling out, 'wait for me!' We also went fishing with our friends, Harold and Eva, on the Mount Bold Reservoir, which was not open to the public but Harold was the forester in charge and had a key for the gate. At night, Gabor, Robbie, and I sometimes went to the Onkaparinga River to fish. Robbie was usually asleep in the van.

With the next vintage we added another wine to our list. This was the Rosza, a dry rose from a blend of Grenache, Shiraz, and Cabernet juice taken right off the skins.

In February 1974, we had a visit from the writer of the wine column of the *National Times* along with his family. It was a very hot day. We had just packed the car for a fishing trip but this was an excellent surprise.

I refreshed the four children and organised cold drinks for everybody while the men talked about the winery and started some wine tasting. Kevin wrote a half-page article for the *National Times* and really put us on the map (see article on the next page). We didn't only have visitors from interstate; they came from all over the world. Our visitor book had entries in French, German, Hungarian, Japanese, and Chinese. The customers came from all walks of life—politicians, ambassadors, the Australian cricket team, the US Air Force from Woomera, and private customers like artists, health-conscious people and wine lovers in general. The response was overwhelming. Visitors lined up all the way along our driveway and around the whole property. We had to have help with the labelling and in the sales area.

Natural wines — made the old Hungarian way in McLaren Vale

In many ways wine, especially in Australia, is still one of the most natural products, with the use of chemical agents kept to a minimum.

Yet a recent experience at McLaren Vale in South Australia when I had the chance to taste a great enthusiast's "natural" wine showed how much the sulphuring and balancing and giving and bacteriostatics of modern winemaking make their presence apparent.

Mr and Mrs G. Berenyi at their small McLaren Flat winery are dedicated to the faithful reproduction of rich, alcohol-heavy wines in the authentic Hungarian tradition.

Not, Mr Berenyi hastens to say, in the current Hungarian style where modern collectives have taken over the wine industry and made it much like any other land's wine.

The Berenyis mean the historic Hungarian way of making, which I suppose gets back to the older French ways too — when wines had to look after themselves against bacterial invasion and other unfriendly acts.

Wines were made once without sulphur (to kill vinegar and other bacteria) and without all manner of sprays on the vine and its berries.

The tending of the fruit was careful and loving; grapes were grown and crushed in clean surroundings and pure air. Many of our modern safeguards, in a whole range of food processes, are a defence against our own pollution.

It is interesting then to taste the Berenyi wine made from unsprayed fruit, pressed and matured without chemical aids.

The character is quite different from any other wine on the Australian scene — soft, gentle, clean, and yet clearly very potent.

There is no doubt that such a wine comes from grapes, and wine grapes of the highest excellence.

Without being too romantic about it all, I found this wine calling up many half-remembered phrases from readings on classical wines of Roman days and of Bordeaux wines of the seventeenth and eighteenth centuries (when the famous Haut-Brion was often printed in English as "Ho Brion").

In present days, one or two great Barolo wines from Italy have this same noble and "uncluttered" feeling.

You may not, on drinking them, become nearly so excited as myself, but I think these natural wines are an experience you should add to your armoury.

The Berenyi husband-and-wife team (winemaking married couples are becoming a McLaren tradition with the Pauls, the Lloyds, and the Pridhams) leave their fruit on the vine much later than usual so that at picking the grapes have a high Beaume.

This sugar is then converted by the grapeskin's native yeasts (no cultured yeasts are used) into an unusually high alcohol wine.

30 degrees proof

I suppose in local wine history only some of the great Rutherglen wines would ever have been made in this way; Rutherglen's natural yeasts, in the "bloom" of the grapeskins, were (and doubtless still are for anyone courageous enough to use them) apparently capable of going to 30 degrees proof easily.

This is the figure the Berenyis seem able to get, or very close to it.

A wine with this amount of alcohol is a hard one to misuse.

All the fermenting is done in wood at the Berenyi winery, and after fermentation the wine is racked into puncheons and sealed for six months.

Usually such wood treatment would give a high oak tannin to the finish of the wine; all I can say is that in the red wine the tannin does not come out this way at all.

If anything, the impression is that of gentle grapeskin tannin, highly agreeable.

Although the actual Berenyi vineyard is only 13 acres or so, they luckily have a few local grape growers willing to grow their grapes the Berenyi way.

Thus increasing gallonages can be made each year, but however much the output at the moment, it is not enough.

When I called, no white wine was available of the

1972 bottling. And to my disappointment, only very few cases of the red. My remarks therefore only apply to my tastings of the red.

If you get in line now and order, the 1973 bottlings will be available around March or April this year.

Prices are $1.50 a bottle, which could rise perhaps ten cents by April, but a mixed case of red and white will certainly do you little damage at that old-fashioned sort of cost.

Natural-food people are, of course, big buyers of the Berenyi products, but to my mind they are of real interest to us all, and will — for keen wine buffs — raise many a challenge.

The address is G. and G. Berenyi Winery, Blewitt Springs Road, McLaren Flat, SA, 5171. And I hope you're in time.

Wine . . . the natural way starts with careful and loving treatment of the fruit.

THE NATIONAL TIMES, JANUARY 28—FEBRUARY 2, 1974

A few days after that, Robbie disappeared. I was in a state of panic. We called him and searched the property but couldn't find him for over an hour, in spite of the help of neighbours. Finally, I discovered him between two big vine bushes with his plastic gun. He put his finger on his lips and shushed me. He was hunting rabbits!

In October of that year, we had another Bushing Festival. Our winery was well-known by then. There were more publications about our wines in *The Australian* and Len Evan's *Complete Book of Wines*.

We received a formal invitation for the Bushing Festival dinner and had a wonderful time. I wore a Russian style black dress with a red inlay on the front and gold and white stitching—a gift from my husband which was much admired.

We increased our production again and bought two white concrete tanks for storage and some grapes from neighbours who grew their grapes without chemicals. Our neighbours also helped with our picking. It was a wonderful team effort.

In spite of the incredible success in the business, our marriage started to break up. At one stage I had a discussion with Gabor about the way his father treated his mother. I said, 'your father treated your mother like a dog'. Gabor hit me for that. I didn't move but thought, *you'll regret that* and the idea of a divorce first formed. Nothing happened in the bedroom. We started living in different rooms.

I felt lonely and sometimes cried—hiding in the vineyard where my dog or Robbie would find me and bring me back to reality. However, we still made plans for a wine cellar—built into the hill. I had a promise from the bank manager for a loan of $50,000 with the security of our stock value of nearly $120,000.

Whereas the several Lords, Knights & Barons of the Royal Domains in the South, being in tenure of divers vineyards & having various Monasteries which maketh wine & meade within their gift, have proclaimed the second Bushing of their Wines in this year of Grace A° D' 1974.

And whereas the aforesaid do verily pledge to turn their energies to sport & jollities in celebration of this joyous event...

THEIR MAJESTIES THE KING & QUEEN OF THE BUSHING do crave the company of...

Squire and Lady Berenyi

at a Bacchanalia of Revels & Feasting within the Great Hall of TATACHILLA commencing at dusk on Saturday the 2nd day of November in this same year of Grace.

To delight the entourage savage Pipers of Celtic origin will herald the wines & meads served to help the company enjoy the ensuing bawdy drolleries. Minstrels of the Court will play as Fools & Jesters, & Jugglers from foreign lands will entrance the throng. Buxom & saucy wenches & mendicant Friars will regale the guests with a copious feast of Beef, Foule & other Meats, & the succulent local fruits & herbs.....

With such bawdy gathering & as the very season decrees venal diversion BISHOPS will attend to grant indulgences & dispensations to the Revellers

Come fill the cup & in the fire of Spring
Your winter garment of repentance fling
'Midst Southern wines by summer dressed
We'll see both Wine & Maker blessed

Misquotat" of Bards both Ancient & Anon.

Given under the Bushing Seal.

But things never went smoothly. We had another bush fire. This time it came from the north and threatened to burn through very high grass in the orchard next door. I was alone again. Gabor was away with Robbie. I still had a chance to hose down the north side of the weatherboard house, but this time the fire brigade put the fire out before it reached our place. Our friend, Harold, left his work to help because he sensed that I was in danger.

1975 was a very special year. We were invited to several historic functions by the government. One of them was the introduction of the plans for the Multi-Function Polis (MFP) called Monarto. Monarto is in the South Australian mallee country, about 60 km east of Adelaide on the eastern foothills of the Mount Lofty Ranges down to the River Murray. It was a dream of the Dunstan government to solve the problem of the sprawling suburbs and create a city of the size of Canberra. Two hundred thousand people were to live in a space-age techno polis, telecommuting to work from homes powered by solar energy and wind, travelling by driverless cabs on electric pathways.

I thought it was a dream with so much foresight. I imagined the city while we were touring the land acquired by the government in 1970 and planted with trees since 1973. Farmers had been compensated and most happily left their farms.

The project received a fund of AU$ 10.5 million from the federal government.

Unfortunately, the plan was abandoned by the Tonkin government after a cost blow out of AU$ 28 million. Now most of the land has been taken over by the zoo for breeding endangered species and other parts have been sold back to farmers.

This was followed by another exciting event. Our friends from the US Air Force in Woomera invited us to the rocket range. A friend flew us in his Cessna to the Woomera airstrip. We had a wonderful time and stayed overnight after listening for three hours to CDs from other friends in the US, who had already returned to the States. We heard music with earphones from four-way speakers. It was like the music was in my head. What an overpowering sound!

The next day we celebrated Independence Day and watched the most extraordinary fireworks I had ever seen and I have seen plenty. The connection to the people there was very special. Unfortunately, this was not the case with my husband. I was filled with happiness and a sense of being part of more than my family.

There was excitement in the winery, too. We made our first port—a natural, unfortified port with 22% alcohol, which aroused considerable interest.

It wasn't long after that Harold came for a visit to the winery. Gabor was in Adelaide and Robbie at the child care centre. On this day we talked the first time about our marriages. We were both extremely unhappy. Eva, Harold's wife, said to me on one of our fishing trips, 'I wish I knew what Harold's plans are, so I can get on with my life'. I gathered then that not everything was as it seemed. We decided there must be something better in life than what we were experiencing. When I told Harold that I loved him since I first met him ten years earlier, we fell into each other's arms and Harold said, 'why didn't you tell me?' Well, we were both married. We kissed for the first time. It was an immediate strong bond. We promised to keep in contact and opened a post box each. I did not feel guilty about this because I was not the one who destroyed his marriage.

After he left I became aware that Kurt had died at the same time that I met Harold the first time at the fiftieth birthday party of friends in our first year in Australia. They were both fifteen years older than me.

A little later, Harold invited us to a fishing trip to the Mont Bold Reservoir. To my greatest surprise, he asked Gabor for my hand in a very graceful manner. Gabor happily agreed, he didn't know how to handle our marriage any more.

Harold and I filed for divorce. In September that year, we went on a holiday together. I experienced the first orgasm in my life—without sex—just a lying on of a hand.

We went to Pt Lincoln and bought ourselves wedding rings and spoke our vows in an Anglican church—marrying ourselves secretly on 10 September 1975. We had such a blessed time and made everyone around us happy, too. At one stage we played a soccer game on a table at a delicatessen. We were so enthusiastic; it became infectious and caught quite an audience. Everybody seemed to be happy with us.

We returned home after a week. I went by plane, Harold by car. I was met at the airport by Gabor and Robbie. It was a very difficult encounter. But I soon got back into the life in the winery. We had more good publicity, an article in the *Southern Vineyards Sketch Book* and two publications by Len Evans in his *Australian Complete Book of Wines*.

Southern Vineyards Sketchbook 1976 - Author V M Branson,
Sketch by Bill Walls.

BERENYI WINERY, McLAREN FLAT

The Berenyi family made wine from their vineyards in Bacska-Banat in the sixteenth century. Successive generations remained secure in their peaceful surroundings until the first World War. Nothing was sacred thenceforth in war-torn Europe and, after hostilities had ceased, their property fell into Yugoslav hands.

Gabor Berenyi's father settled in Sgezed, Hungary, where he again planted his vines and managed a neighbouring estate and winery. Of the family, young Gabor was the only child who only showed an interest in his father's calling, and by the time the boy left home in 1947 to work, first in Austria and then in Germany, he had learnt all the techniques of traditional Hungarian wine-making. It was not until 1969, when he came to McLaren Flat, that he was able to put these skills into practice. In partnership with his wife. In partnership with his wife, Gisela, ten acres of vines were planted.

Berenyi was warned that the land on which he established his vineyard was too sandy. The majority of growers in the Southern Vales prefer a limestone or ironstone base. Gabor was experienced in producing grapes on a sandy terrain and the high quality of his fruit proved his decision to be right. He does not use chemical sprays on his vines but attacks disease with biological fungus, and no chemicals are added in the process of wine-making.

He built his winery and produced his first vintage of 400 gallons in 1970. He exercises special care in the crushing, eliminating any impurities which tend to creep in at this vital period, contending that troubles arise from stalks and other dross and not from anything inherent in the pure juice. The grapes are allowed to ripen fully, which increases the alcohol content and gives a delightful fruity flavour to the wine.

Some of his neighbours now grow their crops the Berenyi way and so he is able to draw additional supplies from them.

To their first vintage, which the Berenyis named McLaren Ruby, they added a white which they named McLaren Gold. The wines will last indefinitely and, as time passes, they gradually develop a liqueur character. The Berenyis can now make 20,000 gallons each year, but will not go beyond the capacity of a family concern to produce wine the old Hungarian way. Nevertheless, further varieties of wine are being added to their range.

Business was flourishing. We bought more storage tanks. By the end of the year I stopped taking names of special visitors after I listed 2,000 customers because I couldn't handle any more correspondence. These customers were my friends as well.

In the New Year, I concentrated on my divorce, paying off bills and making arrangements for a financial settlement. I had an excellent offer for my shares in the winery from a wine merchant from Finland. Gabor did not accept this person as a partner because he had a strong personality. Gabor did not want 'another boss', he said. So I settled for much less with a land broker. We agreed that Gabor paid my settlement in four years' time. But then on a trip to an appointment we had an accident. The brakes of our car failed and we ran into another car. Both cars were badly damaged. We had to pay the costs for both of them. I had to find the money for this out of the turnover because there was no other income. That delayed my departure from the winery for a few months.

My divorce was granted after thirteen years of marriage in February 1976. After we left the family court Gabor kissed me like he never kissed me before. He seemed so relieved. I had to stay a few more months in the winery to finalise my side of the business and have my car repaired.

HAROLD

- -

I became seriously ill with bronchitis at the end of May. It was so bad that I couldn't eat and could hardly breathe or move. Harold had bronchitis, too. He still visited me. The illness may have been caused by our separation. Gabor was afraid that I would die and took me to Harold, who lived in a house in a forest by then.

We arrived at Harold's place at night. The light was on. I got out of the car and went to the house. When I entered, Harold dropped his paint brush and met me with open arms and called out, 'oh, my angel!' We were holding each other for a long time before we could talk again. I said, 'I have come to stay.' We fell asleep in the rocking chair that night.

The next day, we went to the chemist and got ourselves some medication for the bronchitis. We recovered within a few days. Then Harold took me to the winery where I collected my private belongings—my warderobe, some pots, my sewing machine, a few paintings, Athena's scroll, photographs and over a hundred wonderful letters from Harold. I left there without money and had no financial support. I went back to Harold's place.

A few days later, Gabor turned up with Robbie and told me Robbie had ordered him to take him to me—he wanted to talk to me. I took Robbie to the forest and held him in a big hug. He asked me why I left him. Unfortunately, I wasn't able to prepare him for our separation because I was so sick and the departure came totally unexpectedly.

I explained to Robbie that I would never leave him but I had to leave his dad. I would build up a new future for us and we would be together again. At the moment I had to find a new job and make some money to be able to do that. Even so, I assured Robbie that I loved him very much and would always be there for him. He was heartbroken and so was I at that moment. The last thing I wanted was to hurt him. We parted feeling very sad but I promised Robbie that I would visit him soon.

Harold had already started an organic market garden in a paddock in the forest. We worked the garden in the morning and at night. I soon found a job in a delicatessen in a shopping centre in the city. I met customers from the winery there, who didn't greet me very favourably. Everybody thought it was my fault that I left the winery.

I wonder who would leave a happy marriage and flourishing business without a valid reason, but this is how Gabor spread the news.

I wasn't happy about the situation and looked for another job. I found a position in an antique business in the middle of the city. The owner was a good teacher. I learned a lot about antiques and was able to do some jewellery repairs. I received a very beautiful silver necklace with a handcrafted pendant of a horse and a dog from him for Christmas.

With our full-time jobs and the garden, Harold and I were getting only four hours sleep a night. We harvested and washed the vegetables in the evenings and shifted the irrigation pipes, sorted and packed things in the morning, and took a load each to the markets on the way to work. Harold delivered the bulk to a local market while I unloaded special varieties at the organic stall in the Central Market.

We had a box in the kitchen where we put our contributions to the cost of living and for purchasing furniture and machinery. Harold bought an organ and composed songs for me.

We were working very hard, but we had lots of love with very strong chemistry and great satisfaction out of our enterprise. It was the first time in my life that I felt complete. My migraines of eight years disappeared completely.

We often had telepathy and called or met each other when our thoughts crossed. Once I sat on a bench in North Terrace and wrote a card to him when he tapped me on the shoulder. Other times I talked about him to my colleague from the antique shop and there he was walking right towards us. He made friends with my boss, too. They had drinks together.

We really got to know each other by doing everything together. Harold was always calm, nothing could rattle him. He was a fascinating mixture of Spanish (his father) and Belgian (his mother, who was Churchill's secretary before he became prime minister).

Our cooking was quite adventurous, too, with recipes from Spain, Belgian, Germany, Hungary, and Australia. It was never the same. Our deep bond with the land and nature as a whole was a strong connection. I often found a lovely bunch of wild flowers on the dinner table.

We loved horses and joined the Strathalbyn Hunting Club, hunting only stuffed rabbits. I was accepted there as Harold's new partner.

We still had time for outings on weekends. Harold loved trips out of the blue with no plan or destination. I had never done anything like that. I always had a plan and knew where I was going but I learned a lot on those trips and it did awaken my sense of adventure again.

In between crops we even had time for short trips like going on a 'milk run' with Ansett Airlines. We were only five passengers and the pilot and stopped on stations in the outback—delivering mail and food, taking on deliveries, and meeting with country people and their wonderful hospitality. We had a stopover in Perth and had just settled in the hotel when a cyclone struck. We watched from the window in the eighth floor. It was a spectacle—people and debris were thrown around and the sea became wild. I was not scared.

Another trip was to Koolan Island Western Australia, where Harold's son was the harbour master, guiding the big Japanese ships in and out of the small harbour. The island was not open to the public, so the inhabitants did not get many visitors. We were spoiled and were given many presents including a live mud crab. We put him in a bucket and went to bed. He got out and came clap, clap into the bedroom. We got hold of him and locked him into the broom cupboard. He got out again and went right under the bed and clung to the power point and was hard to free. Since we didn't get any sleep we decided we might as well cook him. That's what we did and he was delicious!

We went to Darwin from there. It was not long after cyclone Tracy. The sight really shocked us but Darwin recovered quickly with help from all over the country. It was the first time that I met aboriginal people. I enjoyed friendly talks with them.

After a few months, Harold developed a hernia and wasn't allowed to lift. So that work was left to me, including shifting the irrigation pipes at night. I had good company doing that. My black cocker spaniel, Pasha, my white Persian cat, and an owl which looked and behaved exactly like the owl I had in the winery (she was with me when I hung the washing out), were my constant companions.

Harold finally made an appointment for the hernia operation. He was afraid to die because his father died with the same operation at the same age. Harold came through it and recovered at his sister's place for a few days so as not to burden me with any more work.

At the same time he received his financial settlement from the sale of his previous farm. His divorce was still pending the settlement of a maintenance claim by his wife.

I had received a part settlement. We began looking for our own place and found a wonderful farm at Strathalbyn. The large brick and stone homestead with four bedrooms, an office, a very large kitchen with a huge wood stove and a big packing room was very impressive. Apart from the gutters, everything was in excellent condition.

Adjoining the home was a deer paddock and a lake. A creek ran through the two-hundred-acre property with over two metres of topsoil. The land was used for wheat and sheep growing and was run by a manager for fifty per cent of the profit. This would enable us to pay the place off in five years. There was also a copper mine on the property with mining rights of BHP running out.

We didn't have to think twice. This was a dream come true. We signed a contract in both names, but Harold put the deposit down. The settlement was pending the final boundary survey, but we were given permission to move in right away. We shifted everything with cars and a trailer.

We laid a carpet in the lounge, bought a tall bookshelf, a big deep-freeze chest and Harold ordered the gutters. We felt on top of the world.

We had been there for only three weeks when the unthinkable happened. Harold was about to move the last thing from the forest, our tractor.

He loaded it on the trailer of his car. The car stalled on a hill. Harold decided to unload the tractor and started to get it off the trailer when the car began rolling. The brakes of the car were faulty. Harold looked back to check on the car and ran into a cliff. The tractor overturned on top of him. He was killed instantly. A friend was standing by and was not able to help.

I was working at the antique shop at the time. Police came into the shop and broke the news to me. I screamed. It was as if my heart had been ripped out. My colleagues tried to comfort me, but I felt dead inside. They sent me home. It was our first anniversary, 17 June 1977. I had bought a cake and we were meant to celebrate. I left the cake at work and went to Harold's mother. We cried together. She suddenly stopped and said, 'that's enough!' But my tears were still running. She said, 'if it helps you, Harold told me he had the happiest time of his life with you'. It did help, but there was more to it—this day was also the day when Harold's divorce was to be finalised and we wanted to take Robbie into our home. What was left was a great void.

After I found Harold's will and read it to his sister, we discovered I was not included in it. I was shut out of his family at once. We did make a new will in February after we decided that we would leave what we brought into our relationship to our sons and what we built up together to each other. Harold declared, 'you'll get plenty!' I wonder what he meant by that. He did not keep our arrangement.

As if this was not enough, Harold's youngest son, who was also going to live with us, took the funeral arrangements out of my hands. He hired a young priest who didn't know Harold at all and gave a very empty sermon. I was deeply distressed. My wreath of ninety dark red roses went with his coffin to the crematorium.

That night I saw Harold standing by my bedside saying, 'everything will be alright'. I never saw him in my dreams again. I could not imagine things could be alright again. The dreams of my life had been shattered. The only one to say something positive to me at that time was the coroner who called me 'a remarkable woman'.

More was to come. The previous owner of the farm didn't want to continue the contract with me and asked me to move out. I had a contract but no rights. Legal aid would not help me because it was a property matter and I had no money for a court case and no idea where to go.

The manager of the antique shop told me her son had a house for sale and I could stay there until it was sold. I collected some of my personal belongings, which the officers from the Executive Trustees allowed me to take after they searched our whole house, and I moved into the offered place. Then the house I moved into was sold within a week. I was homeless again.

Harold's sister wouldn't even ask me into her big house when I called on her. Then I asked my sister if I could stay with her until I found another place. After a week she asked me to find a job and move out.

That was too much. I took my car and went on an aimless drive— jolting over a creek, driving through mud and over paddocks, and finally stopping under an olive tree, where I sat for a long time—not making sense of life anymore.

At last I decided to go back to my sister's place, but didn't know where I was and how to get there. I drove towards the city and stopped at a delicatessen. A young couple came out. I told them I was lost and what had happened. They asked where I wanted to go. I gave them my sister's address. They promised to take me there. I followed their car. I was so grateful but had nothing on me to give them. I could only thank them.

I didn't go inside. After a long time my sister came out and asked me to come in.

The next morning I had no idea where I was and what I was doing there. My sister called an ambulance. I was taken to a hospital and then transferred to a psychiatric hospital without understanding what was happening. They told me I had severe depression and I was put in intensive care. I felt totally numb.

My nephew washed my car which was covered in mud.

LIFE WITH BIPOLAR

- -

was put on medication. Sometime later, I had a long talk with the doctor, a psychiatrist, who asked me many questions about my family, my childhood, occurrences of depression in the family, and my relationships with Gabor and Harold. He diagnosed the illness as manic depressive disorder, now known as bipolar disorder or psychosis, which would require long term treatment. He said that it was highly likely that I inherited the illness from my parents.

Nothing puzzles and often frightens people more than the onset of illness in a body or mind that was seemingly healthy before. Many doctors came to know the disease as mania alternating with melancholia. The illness was called manic-depressive illness until 1980 when the name was changed by the American Psychiatrists Association to bipolar disorder.

The cause of the illness is disputed. Some experts say the illness is caused by bad parenting, negative thinking or over-emotional reaction to stress. Others think bipolar is the imbalance in brain biochemistry. All of them classify the illness as mental illness.

My episodes with bipolar were caused by traumas like loss, grief, rejection, and stigma or having no purpose in life. The reaction to these traumas is probably caused by my high sensitivity and has very likely psychological reasons from childhood experiences. Genetics could be a factor, too, and copying parents may also play a role. All this can lead to negative thinking, which can cause the biochemistry in the brain to change.

The change of chemistry is responsible for the symptoms of bipolar. That does not mean it is a mental illness. A total x-ray of my head in later years revealed that I had no damage or deterioration of my brain. Traumas, hurt feelings—emotions and the turmoil of my 'soul' were causing the symptoms. From my experience, bipolar is an illness of the soul. The soul is conceived as an immortal, immaterial entity of a person—the core of thought, action, and morality. My soul has been hurt a lot.

The symptoms of the illness when in a depressed state are:

    no feelings (numb) or tears
    nothing is of interest
    can't enjoy anything
    feeling worthless, hopeless, and helpless
    sensitive to criticism or rejection
    irritable, impatient, aggressive or just
    worrying about global affairs or health problems.

Reactions to these feelings are:

    Hibernation, withdrawal
    Lethargy
    Agitation
    Insomnia or sleeping much more than normal
    Concentration and memory difficulties
    Thinking negatively (negative interpretation of events)

Distrustful (others are against the patient)
Thoughts of suicide

Symptoms of mania are:

Inflated self-esteem or grandiosity
More talkative than usual
Flight of ideas
Decreased sleep
Irresponsible spending
Excessive urge for excitement

I had all of those symptoms at different stages.

The cause of my illness was never identified or even looked for. It was just related to Harold's death but I was not treated for grief and sadness. No counselling was available, just medication for the symptoms of my illness. The medication included lithium carbonate, chlorpromazine, haloperidol, benztropine, thyroxin, and diazepam.

When I was asked how I felt, I couldn't answer that. I wasn't aware of any feelings.

Later, I felt ashamed of being in such a hospital because my family thought I was weak. Harold's family was told by the hospital staff that I would be unlikely to manage my own affairs because of the severity of my illness. All my relationships—family, friends from work, and acquaintances were affected by my illness and they withdrew.

While I was in hospital, I was notified that my property would be sold. I asked for Harold's organ to be handed to me as Harold used to compose songs for me and play it at night. This request was denied.

I was released from hospital after four weeks. With the help of a taxi driver I found a flat in Klemzig. The taxi driver returned after a while and brought me a television set, which he didn't use anymore. I was so grateful for all his help. He was a real Samaritan.

I also was given help from my favourite department store. I visited the finance department and told them what had happened to me. They advanced me AU$ 2,000 for the most needed furniture, without any security, and allowed me to pay it back when I could afford it.

Then I went to the cemetery to visit Harold's grave, only to find out his body was still in the morgue and no arrangements for a burial had been made. I was shocked. It seemed Harold's family took the inheritance and forgot about him. I made arrangements for a cremation, which he wanted, and bought a site in the Rose Garden for him. The ashes were buried a few days later.

This was all too much. I had no support. Nobody wanted to know me. I relapsed into my illness and was readmitted to the hospital. There I had positive feedback from other patients. We formed a discussion group of four patients—two male and two female. The outstanding person in our group was Robert, an engineer. We talked about anything— religion, philosophy, medication problems, the doctors, and so on. The positive atmosphere we created in the hospital was not hidden from the doctors. One day, we were given permission for a walk outside the hospital. We ended up in a restaurant and enjoyed prawns and champagne and returned in a happy mood.

After ten days, I left for home again. I decided I would change my name since I was not lucky with men and wanted to start a new life. A job was advertised for a secretary at a butcher shop and I applied. I was employed but my desk was next to the hanging carcasses and the smell was unbearable.

I was only there for ten months when I received an offer to go to Coober Pedy to learn opal cutting and selling. I accepted this offer because it would take me away from all the traumas and I could pursue my creative ambitions.

I drove to Coober Pedy in my V8 Monaro, which I had exchanged for my Valiant because the Valiant kept causing problems with tuning, brakes, the radiator, and so on. On my arrival, the opal miner who hired me had to settle a dispute with the neighbour over machinery. I was alone in the accommodation when two scruffy men arrived and wanted my opals. I told them I had just arrived. They were quite forceful but finally left because I repeatedly assured them I had no opals. I was pretty shaken and decided to go back to Adelaide the next day. I went to my sister's place. She had arranged for my furniture to be stored in the shed of her next door neighbour.

I tried to find a job for two days but the job situation was hopeless. I decided that I would return to Germany. I gave the Monaro to Gabor and organised a trip to Germany. I didn't really feel I belonged anywhere.

I arrived at my mother's place and she allowed me to stay. I found a job in a supermarket within a week and paid board to my mother. After three months, I applied for a position in the public service, the Health Board, my last working place in Germany. I was accepted because of my excellent record for an appointment in the personnel department. I also found a lovely apartment near my workplace. I was expected to get acquainted with the legislation and regulations for all personnel within a fortnight. There were many complex rules, and for me, were hard to comprehend, after being without contact with law and administration for twelve years.

I ended up again with a breakdown. I was using inappropriate language and wanted to start an Easter fire with all the laws and regulations. I was, of course, made redundant and I ended up in hospital. I could leave the hospital again after a fortnight, but had to find some work again. I lost my apartment because the landlord did not want a tenant who had been in a psychiatric hospital.

My poor mother took me back into her place. I soon found other employment in a garden centre. I did like the environment with the friendly staff but was still very depressed and suffering from the side effects of my medication. I met numerous English speaking customers. They stayed on in this suburb after the occupation when they took over many of the homes of the rich people. They picked me very quickly for an Australian. I obviously had an Australian accent.

One day, I had a very special customer. He came in with a very attractive lady. They asked me for secateurs. I enquired what they wanted them for. He answered, 'for pruning vineyards'. 'Oh', I said, 'the ones we have in stock are not good enough for pruning vineyards'. He wanted to know what I knew about vineyards. 'Well', I said 'I lost one'.

He became quite intrigued and said to his companion, 'we have to shift this lady'. He then introduced himself as Dr Shabahang from Persia. The lady was the German Ambassador from India. They invited me for dinner to her home the next day. We had appetisers there and then moved to a restaurant where he hired the attic where we could talk without interruption and did we talk. This evening was to become the most exciting experience.

Dr Shabahang revealed he was a baron and lecturer in the Tehran University where he was teaching eight faculties—mathematics, engineering, physics, chemistry, history, and languages. He spoke eight languages, English and German without an accent. He owned large vineyards and previously had also extended coal mines, which were monopolised by the Shah. He wanted me to run the vineyards and supervise the staff. He offered me a large house and time to get used to the new surroundings and language. I raised my doubts that I would learn the language but he waved that away saying, judging by the way I speak English, I would easily learn it. This all seemed like a dream!

We talked through the whole weekend. The restaurant looked after us with food and refreshments. I also learned that Dr Shabahang was working as a scientist and spy in Germany during World War II and belonged to the team which plotted Hitler's assassination. I was totally fascinated by this man. He left for Berlin the next day and promised to keep in contact. Well, that didn't happen. A few days after, Dr Shabahang left, Khomeini had returned to Persia from exile and expropriated the vineyards. That's when the dream ended.

I went back to work in the garden centre. During my vacation, I took a holiday with my mother to Austria. We climbed the highest mountains and my fear of heights was non-existent. We had a wonderful time with excellent weather, stops in Salzburg where Mozart was born, and we visited Hitler's home site—Berghof in Obersalzberg of the Bavarian Alps. The house was demolished by the West German government in 1952, after it had been bombarded during the war, burnt out by the SS and vandalised after the war. But there was no skiing on that trip.

It didn't take long and there was bad news again. My sister in Australia wrote to me that her neighbour had sold her house and the agent told her to get rid of the furniture and contents from the garage. The neighbour did just that without making an effort to contact me. She had my address, I wrote to her twice to find out how much rent she wanted. She never answered but sold or gave away my whole household.

I took that fairly calmly but because of the injustice of it all I decided to return to Australia. I booked my trip. By then I had a very good relationship with the staff at the garden centre. They tried to persuade me to stay but I wanted to rescue as much as I could from my belongings. I left my family and Germany for the second time.

Back in Adelaide, I stayed at my sister's place briefly but soon found a comfortable, furnished flat near the beach. I started investigating what had happened. I contacted the police and found help to locate the woman who had sold my belongings. The police confiscated her savings account of AU$ 750 and located some of the buyers of my furniture.

I visited a young couple who had my teak bedroom suite and the bedding. I felt sorry for them as they had bought it in good faith. They offered me $350 and the bedding back. I had a furnished flat, so I left the suite but I took the bedding. Another couple had my fridge. They didn't pay for it. I reclaimed it because I needed it.

There were a few items left in the garage, a scroll from Athena, a picture of white swans, and a few things for the kitchen. I had to start again after losing nearly everything I owned for the fifth time but there was always something to start with again.

Looking for work again, I was attracted by an advertisement for a franchise in an organic fertiliser factory. I had no money to buy the franchise and offered my mortgage on the winery for security. The owner of the factory talked me out of it. He was very protective. We became friends. He was highly intelligent and a lot of fun to be with. He was previously a representative for Chrysler. He won a gold star for a speech in Detroit, which attracted a lot of business for Chrysler. He presented it to me.

I found a job at a supermarket as dairy manageress. I was only there for a few months when I had an accident lifting heavy boxes from behind a row of other boxes. I cracked a disc and was unable to work. The manager was angry with me and didn't believe that I had really injured myself. I received a worker's compensation and had to settle for a lump sum of $350 and no further employment, in spite of being represented by a lawyer. I bought my son a motorbike, boots, and a leather jacket for that money. Until then he was riding the bike of a neighbour's son. He loved motorbikes.

I offered Gabor help for a renovation of the winery but he adamantly refused.

One day, I had a visit from missionaries of the Mormon Church. I had met these missionaries before, at my first flat following Harold's death when I was playing my first record of a series of the Mormon Tabernacle Choir, which seemed a bit like destiny. I was welcomed into the church again and made some friendly contacts. In spite of that, I had a relapse into my illness, when I was supposed to sit for a test for a job. I was readmitted to the same hospital. When I was released this time, I needed someone to care for me. A member from the church took me into her place. I lived in the tiniest room I'd ever been in. It was smaller than a prison cell. It just had room for the bed, a chair, and a very small wardrobe. I started to drink too much wine. A blood test revealed I had a jaundiced liver. I felt totally out of place. I had to get out of there and I did.

I found a beautiful furnished apartment in North Adelaide and a new employment as a representative with Pieroth German Wines. I loved their wines and could represent them enthusiastically at private wine tastings and shows. I had strong competition with male consultants who didn't want to share the market with me. I hung in there for a year with long country trips to the mid-north and Yorke Peninsula. I enjoyed meeting people with interest in good wines, but in the end the pressure from the male colleagues was too much and I resigned.

During that time, my friend from the fertiliser company had a traumatic experience with threatening people entering his factory, holding him at gunpoint and robbing his records and money. He fled to my place. I lent him my car so he could go about his business undetected. We became very close but parted because he wanted another child (he had a very talented daughter, a teacher, in Japan). I could not fill his dream. That was in 1981.

Following another breakdown, my lawyer achieved the repossession of the winery for me for my outstanding settlement. By that time I was too sick to take advantage of it. It would have involved a huge clean-up operation and investment for replacements. I would also need a winemaker. Apart from that, I was threatened by Gabor that he would shoot me if I did take over the winery. I believed he would.

In 1982, I finally settled with him for the part of the property without buildings, which was cleared from vines, to be sold as a hobby farm. I was able to sell the block and at the same time the Housing Trust organised a lovely two-bedroom penthouse in the centre of Adelaide City for me.

With the money from the block, I was able to buy new furniture for my place and a new car. It had to be a small car, which would run cheaply. I settled for a Ford Laser. It was hard to get used to a small car after my V8s. In the housing estate I met a lady I knew from the apartment building in North Adelaide who was involved in politics. We became good friends. She was a friend of the Queen (she showed me letters) and was called Grand Dame Idina Probyn. Idina lost a fortune in real estate in Victoria. Well, I lost several fortunes before we met. We understood each other. Idina started playing scrabble with me to keep my mind occupied. We also had exciting debates about matters in politics on all levels of government. We both had strong opinions and principles and when politicians annoyed us too much we wrote to them.

When we had the pilot strike in 1989, I wrote to the treasurer Paul Keating and the Prime Minister Bob Hawke about the damage the right to strike has done to Australia and that in Germany the right to strike is legally outlawed for all public service, transport and key positions. For other occupations and trades it has practically become redundant because employees have shares in their company and wouldn't strike against themselves. I emphasised that with our level of education we can settle our disputes in a more civilised manner. Without strikes our productivity will increase, costs will decrease, and everything will work out in favour of our economy and balance of trade. I also remarked that we should encourage loyalty, responsibility, and reliability to build up our reputation in the world.

Mr. Keating thanked me through his private secretary for bringing my views to his attention. After receiving thanks from the Department of the Prime Minister, they sent my letter on to the South Australian State Government to deal with it on state level.

Apart from that, I had a big laugh when I read in the paper that the troops could not get to an important manoeuvre in the Northern Territory because of the pilot strike. They used private planes for the transport of the troops. I wonder what they would do in a case of war.

The person who made the decision to send them by private planes could never have been in a war.

Beside politics, I became interested in the cultural side of life and joined the Festival Theatre, The Art Gallery, and the Zoo and a little later the National Trust. It was all interesting and uplifting but I still experienced another relapse into my illness, a so-called anniversary episode on the date of Harold's death. This was the third time. I was crying for over a week without apparent reason. It was also stated that I didn't comply with my medication.

The fact that this happened should have given the medical profession a sign that my grief had not been addressed, but all they could do was to treat me like a naughty child who didn't take her medicine. I never received any counselling. I frequently asked the treating doctors for advice about what I could do to get over my illness. I had a strong feeling that the medication didn't work for me. All I heard was a stern warning to stay on the tablets. There has never been an attempt by the doctors to find the cause of my illness. All they did was treat the symptoms, which I later found out, could have been caused by the medication (antidepressants!).

Through Centrelink I found work with the education department. I had to learn how to handle a switchboard, which I found very hard. I am not technically minded. I was then introduced to the registry and tertiary assistance sub registry—maintaining files, other registry indexes and registers, conducting file research, and mail clearance. Comments in my report read—I was a conscientious, dedicated worker, capable of any work required without complaint. My help in TEAS Registry was very much appreciated after a little time of training and supervision, but I still didn't qualify for a position.

I wanted to be independent of government support. My applications for various positions were all rejected, mainly because I was on lithium and also because I had been self-employed which could lead to 'problems' with other workers.

I decided to become self-employed again and enrolled in a course for real estate. I loved this because I felt strongly about property after losing two farms. My psychiatrist at this stage, a well-known doctor and in charge of the psychiatric ward in the Repatriation Hospital told me, 'you'll never end up in real estate!' Well, I proved him wrong. I completed the course in the Adelaide College, got a license and *worked* in real estate for six months. I even tried to sell our winery at that time, because Gabor got into financial strife after losing many customers. His wine wasn't the same quality as at the start. I was unsuccessful with the sale. The winery was too neglected.

I discovered the owner of the real estate company I worked for, was very corrupt. He took items out of places he had on the rent list and sold them. I also experienced illegal activities by other companies like removing For Sale signs and replacing them with their own. Male agents stepped in and took over my listings.

I left real estate because of that and went into my own enterprise, a gift shop—*Robin's Treasure Chest*. I researched areas for this kind of business and settled on a rich suburb with hardly any business of this nature. I rented a shop on the main street and got a license. I enjoyed shopping for the opening, finding a lot of unique items from many different wholesalers. Everything was delivered as I had no car. Shopping was done before business hours.

The opening was a champagne celebration with my friends and the return on sales was enough to restock. I increased the range of my merchandise and advertised my specials with flyers in the letter boxes, which I delivered after hours.

During this time, Gabor sold the winery and moved with Robert to Pt Wakefield.

In spite of all my efforts the turnover declined because my main customers were pensioners. The rich people worked in Adelaide and did their shopping there. The overhead became too much after two years and I had to sell the shop. I was fortunate to find a good agent. He sold the shop and I broke even, but made no profit.

But there was one outstanding colleague in my real estate company, a Hungarian baron. We became very attracted to each other. We went on private outings with his Italjet. He later bought a Jaguar to show me off. He was so proud of me, as I was of him, but I couldn't show it like that. We had an incredible time for two years, in spite of him being married and my illness. I had the suspicion he had bipolar, too. He taught me a lot about how to handle people—from his perspective. He committed suicide by shooting himself while in a depression.

His teachings did get me into trouble later because he drew on people in authority. When I mentioned friends in higher places at admissions to hospitals like chancellors in Germany, the premier Don Dunstan or the Hungarian baron, they thought I made this up. I rarely found a doctor who trusted me. I was always treated the same because I had a history of bipolar. It was never checked why the relapses occurred. I was bearing a label.

For a little while I worked in a fruit packer market, but the death of my friend and the loss of my shop and the inability to find suitable work drove me to a suicide attempt with an overdose of lithium in March 1986. My son took me to my doctor, then to the Royal Adelaide Hospital. I was transferred to Glenside. My treatment with medication was not changed and no counselling was given. Lithium doesn't kill. It only blocks the brain and you can't think straight. I was released after a month.

From July to August that year, I attended an accountancy course to improve my employment chances followed by an advertised 'mind power' course, believing that would bring me closer to overcoming my illness. The opposite happened. I went off my medication because I thought positive thinking would overcome my problems.

I went on a high and booked a trip to Stockholm on bankcard (because I thought I would be safe there as it was built on rocks and I suspected we have earthquakes in Adelaide) with a stopover in London to go shopping at Harrods. I became sick on the plane, had a hallucination I was in a shuttle and my friend Robert was the pilot. I shouted, 'crush them, and crush them!' They took me off the plane in Singapore and delivered me to the hospital—against my will—after trying to flee and being caught. I stayed in the hospital for a couple of days—in handcuffs, which I got out of several times. Then they left me alone until a doctor and a security officer took me back to Adelaide and I was admitted to Glenside Hospital, to the Brentwood Ward, which was for violent patients. I was never violent in my whole life! I had a chair thrown at me and there were constant fights.

I was put on chlorpromazine, lithium carbonate, haloperidol, benzhexol and flurazepam. My first thought was to get out of there and I tried to find exits. I was brought in contact with a self-help group. All I learned from them was—I am a loner. Amidst people who believed in psychiatry, I probably was.

I became an outpatient in Flinders Hospital where tegretol was added to my medication which caused stuttering and blocking the brain, so I could not finish a sentence. This practically killed all my self-confidence.

I was without work until April 1988, when I found employment with a prestigious new hotel in Adelaide. I started before the opening and helped prepare the kitchen for the big event. I worked there doing herbs and fruit baskets for special guests until November when I asked for a transfer because I had a problem with my French supervisor who didn't like Germans. After that I worked in different positions as hotel assistant. I was made redundant when visitor numbers dropped drastically. That was a very hard decision because by then my son had decided to live with me and I had to support him.

I received excellent references from the hotel which stated that I was an intelligent woman who could succeed at anything given the right opportunities. Yes, the right opportunities, that's what I was looking for. My education from Germany—five years college—was still not accepted in Australia because there is no comprehensive course like that. To improve my chances further I did a 'Peak Performance Seminar— the Alpha Personal Development Seminar'. It didn't help. Now I was overqualified for most positions.

I badly needed job security, love, and a purpose in life. Work was only the means to pay the bills. My work history was unstable and unsatisfactory. The first thoughts about a goal started to manifest.

I had the deep desire to get over my illness and lead a normal life. That's what made me ignore the side effects of lithium, of feeling like a zombie and not being able to use my memory most of the time. Apart from that, my hands were shaking and I was feeling dizzy. It is very hard to appear normal with that sort of a thing happening.

I had lots of fantasies at that time, like flying to the moon, Mars, and Venus.

Instead of flying to the moon, I drove to the aboriginal settlement for people from Maralinga in Yalata to get to know the original Australians. In 1952, the aboriginals had been moved there from their traditional land which was used for atomic testing by the British program between 1955 and 1963, conducting seven tests. I worked in the roadhouse, where I made good contact with the aboriginal people who lived in appalling conditions. I learned that many people had died there from the effects of alcohol since they had been removed from Maralinga.

The camp for aboriginal people was built between two pubs and, above all, the Lutheran 'mission' had a liquor license. I was disgusted, not only about government planning (I had the impression it was done on purpose) but also because of the fact that the owner of the roadhouse collected artefacts from the aboriginal people for a pittance and sold them by the truckload in Sydney for inflated prices. He felt that I was on to his schemes and sacked me with the words, 'you don't belong here, you should work in a fashion shop', which was not my intention at all.

I went home, but I visited the Aboriginal and Torres Strait Islander Social Justice Commissioner. I was not particularly welcome—I was white! So I stayed at the doorway and said, 'I have a message for you. You are entitled to compensation for your land in Maralinga. Claim it!' I know many other people in the community were urging them to seek justice for the damage to their land. They did win their case but not for what it was worth.

On the fifth of May 1989, Peter Hackett from *The Advertiser* took up their plight with an article 'Conditions in Yalata—a disaster' replying to a study by Prof Donald Cheek, which stated that extreme malnutrition among Yalata children between six and thirteen years are at least one year behind in their body height and weight. The conditions in Yalata were described as the worst for any aboriginal settlement. I took the matter further by writing to the Minister for Aboriginal Affairs, Mr Hemming, describing the poor quality of food served in the Roadhouse where a lot of the aboriginals ate, the lack of education about cleanliness, budgeting, and gardening, apart from other education which should have been pursued by the 'mission'.

I recommended that the settlers be shifted away from the pubs to the land where they did their artwork. The minister took three months to reply to my letter. He promised to introduce legislation on alcohol consumption and sale in Yalata but did not agree with the health concerns, he made out they did not exist. I handed a copy of his letter to the Aboriginal Legal Right Movement and they forwarded it to their lawyers.

I also sent a complaint to the head office of the Lutheran Church and declared that I did not want to be associated with a church which allowed so much negligence and sold alcohol to people who could not handle it. I resigned from the church.

My shortest employment led to a lot of activities and made me feel there were still people who needed me.

In April that year, I got a call from my mother after she had just taken an overdose. I screamed! I couldn't help her after we had finally achieved a lovely relationship for the last two years. My youngest sister came to the phone. I told her what happened (she had just arrived home) and asked her to take my mother to a hospital in a hurry. My mother died three weeks later. My private psychiatrist said to me in a consultation soon after that 'I would end up like my parents'. Assumptions, assumptions! This was *a wonderful outlook for my future.*

It nearly happened. One day, suddenly, my whole surroundings turned black. I took an overdose of thyroxin. My son took me to my doctor and she made me walk to the hospital (RAH) alone! They transferred me to Fullarton—unconscious. When I became conscious again I felt I had extraordinary powers. They were soon reduced to very little on further medication. I was very well cared for—quite a change from Glenside—and could return home after eleven days.

My efforts to explore every possible avenue, which may lead to suitable employment never eased. I was very unhappy to depend on the government for my living. I offered to work with street kids. I had experiences from the Youth Board in Germany. It didn't take me long and I got into trouble again after successfully training as counsellor for service to youth. I noticed that there were several organisations involved in the same work and thought they could be much more effective as one organisation with combined power. I actually talked to a couple of people in other organisations about this. When the leader of my group heard about that, it ended my job.

But volunteer work was plentiful. The next assignment I had was as a tutor for migrant education in Adelaide. I had interesting eager students, a doctor and his wife from Vietnam and an Italian couple. The doctor and his wife were soon employed (I wasn't). The Italian couple wanted to keep me forever. They cooked for me and we studied the language while we were cooking and learned the words for everything around us—like I used to learn English when I arrived here. It was fun.

Another enjoyable position was in the archaeology department of the South Australian Museum, where I worked in the Aboriginal Family History Unit as a volunteer. My duties included working with archival materials relating to the Norman Tindale Collection of genealogies and photographs taken on the Harvard Adelaide University Expedition 1939/53/54. This included establishing files for copy negatives taken from each state in Australia, where they had been collected, numbering the negatives and inscribing names, age, sex, location, and dates on the reprints.

I photocopied genealogies from various states and arranged them in folders. I also typed forms and other relevant information and history of the tribes important for the unit's operation.

I was very much appreciated for my work and recommended as being a very willing, conscientious worker who showed initiative, had a reliable character, was well—mannered and meticulous in appearance and could be trusted to work on her own, but I didn't get the position I worked in when it became available. A person with university degree was selected instead.

I was tired of applying for jobs and applied to do a writer's course at the Adelaide College. I didn't pass the test. My writing lacked imagination. I was in a depressed state, which doesn't exactly encourage creativity. Well, I was fortunate. One of the two teachers who tested me was a customer from our winery and remembered my hospitality. He emphasised that the story of that winery should be told. He talked the other teacher into letting me pass. I did learn a lot about technical requirements, copyright, publishing, and so on.

I translated an information booklet for my dentist from German to English, which he greatly appreciated.

Finally, I found some challenging paid work with an insurance company through work experience with Centrelink as an accountant. I had to learn accountancy on the computer and insurance law. However, I didn't accomplish touch typing. I never liked typing. I had four secretaries in my last position in Germany because I could produce so much work. I was able to do the accountancy work and even solved some legal problems.

One day, my son came to the office—dirty, bare footed, and demanding. He seemed to be on drugs. My neighbour gave him my work address. I was dismissed the next day in January 1992. I was well-liked by then and was presented with a huge flower arrangement in a tall vase when parting.

The relationship with my son was strained. He was influenced in such a negative way against me by his father and behaved like a rebel, often getting into the wrong company and into mischief. He had no respect for me or anybody else. We made rules, which he had to keep and it was agreed that if he broke them he had to move out. He grew marijuana in his bedroom. When I discovered it, I asked him to get rid of it. He promised. I saw the plants again and gave him an ultimatum. He told me he had disposed of them. When I checked, they were still there. I thought he needed a stronger lesson and called the police, assuming they had rehabilitation facilities. The police didn't know what to do. They finally collected the plants and locked Robbie up for the night. When he came back, I learned there are no rehab facilities for drugs. This whole experience didn't improve my relationship with Robbie. He moved out.

By that time there was a drug problem with the tenants on the ground floor where people with paraplegia lived. They not only used drugs, they were dealing with them, which caused a lot of traffic.

All these negative influences caused my next breakdown. One day, I ordered a taxi and asked the driver to take me to Strathalbyn. I wanted to see our farm again. The driver took me there. The farm was subdivided. None of our dream left. The driver took me home where I discovered I couldn't pay him. He drove me for two hours. He was furious. At last we reached an agreement that I pay the fare off. The state of my mind got worse and I ended up in hospital again, where I stayed a whole month.

After that, I was cared for privately by the psychiatrist, who treated me in hospital, and community outreach. Home again; I contacted my psychiatrist to get his permission to travel to Germany. He thought it would be a good idea. Within days I had my trip booked and my family notified.

It turned out to be the best thing what could have happened to me. My family, especially my youngest sister, welcomed me warmly. They spoiled me and made me feel really loved. I never had had such a good time with my family before and I felt where my roots really were.

I returned home after three weeks. I seemed to be myself again. I asked the Housing Trust for a transfer to another accommodation to get out of the drug traffic atmosphere of the place I lived in. They were really good to me and found a beautiful townhouse for me in a nearby suburb.

Just after I moved there my brother and his wife came for a visit from Germany. I met them at the airport where I also met my sister and her husband, who I hadn't seen for years. I wanted to renew our relationship but she refused. My brother went to her place as they had arranged previously. They came to visit me one day. I couldn't even spoil them. I was broke after my removal to the townhouse, but we had a fairly good time.

A little later, I found a paid job as a cleaner in the taxation department.

It was a steady job. I had to clean the exchange and computer rooms.

After a few months, the department decided to build a new computer room. It had a tiled floor. They moved the computers in before it was cleaned. I was asked to remove the glue from the joints of the tiles, but was not allowed to use steel wool or other harsh methods because that would interfere with the computers. That meant I had to do it with plastic sponges.

I needed a lot of pressure with my hands which affected my elbows and also my knees. I suffered from severe pains. The department offered me knee pads! That didn't ease the pain. I had to see a doctor who gave me a sick certificate and suggested I contact Workcover. The taxation department refused to pay any compensation.

So I went to a law firm, which took up my case, but the firm made deals with the department and treated me like a disease because they found out I was on lithium. Finally, Workcover rang me and asked whether

I would settle for $12,000. I agreed, even so I should have asked for a year's wages because I would be unable to work for at least that long.

My lawyer charged me fees for the settlement, which I arranged. She refused to drop the fees. There was nobody who could help me in this matter because lawyers don't fight lawyers.

By then my son was living with me again and this time it worked out. He told me that he had heard there were cheap houses for sale in Peterborough. He knew I wanted to have my own place again. The first time in many years I had a goal. While I was thinking about this opportunity, I helped Robbie to get a flat from the Housing Trust, pointing out that he suffered from depression and needed a two-bedroom place so I could stay with him when he was ill. He was given a nice place in a lovely area.

On New Year's Day, 1994, a state-wide bush fire broke out in New South Wales. I was shocked by the photographs I saw in the news on television and offered to volunteer with support work. I organised collections of food, clothing, and household items and helped with transport arrangements. The organisations I was involved with—the New South Wales Government, Suburban Transport Services Adelaide, and the Salvation Army sent me unexpected awards of appreciation for outstanding contribution during the devastating fires. I treasure these awards. I finally received recognition for my voluntary work.

A few months later, I found some interesting voluntary work in the Citizens Advice Bureau in Adelaide, where I updated files for their vast information system—manually or with the computer. I was called a responsible worker, adjusting well to people and different tasks and recommended for any position I applied for. My self-confidence started to return. What a difference from the judgments in most psychiatric hospitals. There, patients are treated as if they don't have any rights and are in a very low class. The psychiatric personnel have no idea of the feelings of their patients, unless they have a mental illness themselves, they wouldn't know what it feels like to be out of control and be controlled by others. That's why they make, sometimes, very cruel decisions.

I felt stronger now and could overcome side effects of the tablets. I started to make plans and new contacts. I became involved in a German travel organisation, *Boefa,* through the German Club. We accommodated German visitors and showed them our beautiful city. I wrote travel stories for their magazine. It gave me the chance to meet wonderful people, who kept in contact with me for some time. I also joined the UFO Club. I am fascinated by the UFO phenomenon. I believe I saw the first one in World War II, two from the vineyard and one in Coober Pedy.

Early in 1995, I went to Peterborough and checked out the real estate market. I didn't find a place which I could call home at my first visit, but I had a wonderful tour guide, the owner of a historic museum, who showed me all the hidden treasures of Peterborough for four hours. I couldn't possibly pay for his generosity and enthusiasm. I told him that on my next visit I would bring him a beautiful doll for his exquisite doll collection in the museum.

The real estate agent kept in contact. A few weeks later, he invited me back to have a look at his new listings. This time destiny opened new ways. I stayed with a couple from Adelaide in a hotel and we talked about our plans in Peterborough. I told them I was looking for a house. They were just touring. Since I brought my doll along, I intended to see the tour guide first.

When I arrived at his museum, he was talking to the couple from the hotel, discussing houses for sale. I presented him with my doll (Giselle).

SHADOWS OVER THE SUN

Then there was the big surprise. The owner of the museum had a house for sale adjoining his backyard.

I fell in love with it on sight. It was a large stone-brick house. I had a dream about a stone house. Going inside, it was fully renovated, painted in my favourite pastel colours most suited for all my pictures. The ceiling had a decorated centre rose and ornate cornices. The floors were shining red jarrah timber. The bathroom had a large bath and shower and newly tiled walls. There were three bedrooms, a sunroom, and a large kitchen.

I was impressed. It was better than my dream, but I was sure I couldn't afford it. It had only been on the market one week, for $40,000. I said I could not afford more than $36,000. The owner suggested seeing the agent to discuss the situation. The agent wasn't very helpful at the beginning. He wouldn't believe that the owners would sell the house for my offer and called them. He got the okay. Then he asked me to contact the finance company he was dealing with. Because of my good deposit they arranged a loan within a day over the phone, with my pension the only security. I would never have been given a mortgage as a pensioner in Adelaide.

The contract was signed and the mortgage approved on the fourth of May 1995. Arrangements for the removal followed with the local removalist agreeing to shift me on 29 May. I could have gone on 27 May, but that was my wedding day with Gabor and the date of four removals, which never turned out to be very lucky. I watched the ballet *Giselle* again, instead.

Packing and moving was fun this time. I drove to my first home in my own name in the front of the truck of the removalist. We talked about people choosing to live in Peterborough. There were retirees, who sold their expensive houses in Adelaide or other cities to buy a cheaper house and live on their savings. There were others who stayed a while and then moved back to the city, but returned again. Peterborough has some sort of magic attraction.

Moving into my house was a wonderful experience. I took my time to arrange the furniture, hang the pictures, and add some knick-knacks. I was so happy, for the first time, since my battle with bipolar. I hadn't been sick for three years. Nobody knew about my illness in Peterborough. I had a new start, but was still on medication.

My new home.

PETERBOROUGH

- -

After I had my home organised, I went to the District Council of Peterborough to find out if there was a way to green the town. It is a desert town but the soil does grow trees. There were very few around. We established a contact with *Trees for life*. I had a few months before the first seeds, boxes and soil arrived.

I used the time to join courses at TAFE for *Trades for women* and started the first term in the horticulture centre and established my garden. There was a large chook yard, which I didn't need and pulled down. I wanted to grow vines around the fences and across the yard and planted rare cuttings of old vines from the established *Seven Hill* winery which is run by monks. The cuttings took well.

My garden harboured a variety of fruit and almond trees, which all needed pruning. One day, I was sitting in a huge almond tree cutting off a big, dry branch. I went down with it in spite of holding on to the branch I was sitting on. I fell hard—six feet—and was hurt. I couldn't move, let alone get up. Neighbours next door saw what happened and rushed over to help. They lifted me up and walked me slowly into the house, where I sat down on the couch. The neighbours thought I would be alright and left but I was in agony. I moved slowly to the phone and called the ambulance. They came quickly and drove me ever so carefully to the nearby hospital.

The consulting doctor thought I had bruised kidneys and was waiting for a sign of blood, which did not occur. So he sent me home after three days. I still could hardly move. It took some time before I could carry on with my normal duties.

Finally, the boxes for 2,000 trees arrived from *Trees for life* and I could begin my propagating program. I put the boxes on top of my underground tank to keep them away from any creepy-crawlies. I also started collecting herb cuttings and potted them for future sales. The garden, which still contained virgin soil, was ideal for growing things. The huge almond trees offered shelter and the necessary shade. Everything started flourishing.

The first lot of tree seedlings went to the Council (free of charge) for plantings on the streets leading into Peterborough, and on reserves, and around the train station. For the second plantings the Council made me some benches from the pipes of pulled down mesh fences at the right height for me to work the seedlings comfortably standing up. The second lot went to the Council as well for further greening of the town. After that I received permission to sell the trees to farmers, the meat works and even interstate but *Trees for life* no longer supplied me with seeds and boxes. I found my own suppliers and got the boxes from a supermarket.

My backyard began to look like a nursery. I had to find an outlet for what I was growing and I found a friend who took me and my goods to the Peterborough market as I had no car. Another friend from the horticulture centre took me to other markets in surrounding towns, which was a great help. Word soon spread around. People found me in my garden, too. I also joined the garden club and made new friends.

Another connection came with a local hardware store, where I could sell some of my herbs and shrubs, which I had included in my collection.

My vines started bearing fruit the second year. Things were growing fast. I had to think of a wine cellar. My underground tank was always empty as it had no inlet. It seemed to be the perfect solution. I had a new roof put on to it. A special wooden staircase and door with a blacksmith lock completed the achievement. The furnishings—a large wine rack, two black-leather chairs, a hand-carved table, and a large print of wine and grapes created a beautiful atmosphere.

It took nearly another year to put the first wines—Riesling, Traminer, red and white Frontenac, and cabernet into it. I had a very exciting time making the wine with only basic equipment but not quite like Gabor used to make it—even so the grapes were organically grown. I used yeast for fermentation and milk for filtering. It didn't last very long. The wine was too good and actually quite interesting.

One day, I got a wonderful offer from the postmaster to use his car park for a nursery and move into the vacant apartment, which was suitable for a living area and an office, in the Post Office. I had only accomplished two semesters in the horticulture centre and knew very few species of plants and trees, mainly what I had grown, but I took the offer. Totally new planning had to begin. I had to get a business license and find suppliers for more stock to fill the place. I found several wholesalers who would deliver to Peterborough and send me catalogues and order sheets. Then I had to find a tenant for my house.

Luckily, I won a contract for landscaping two blocks in the retirement village of the Peterborough hospital and made some profit, exactly $200, just as much as I had for the start of the winery in McLaren Flat. It was enough to buy some annuals and shrubs. I had plenty of herbs and trees.

The place was not suitable for storage of fertiliser, chemicals, and tools.

So I called it *Little Garden Centre* and was given the license.

It was a busy time to move the stock and shift my furniture into the apartment. Through an advertisement in the school and hospital, I found a tenant for my house—a music teacher from the high school, who paid just a bit more rent for my partly furnished house than I needed for renting the place at the Post Office. It was all working out fine.

I invited the mayor of the District Council of Peterborough, Ruth Whittle, (who later received the Queens Honour Award for local government and community service twice) to open my nursery. We had become friends through my interest in politics. All my friends, I had a few by then, received invitations and I placed an advertisement in the local paper. It turned out to be a quiet but very relaxed and happy atmosphere. I made my first speech since the winery and I was very excited. I took enough money to buy more stock. I realised it might be hard to convince more locals to buy from me. I was a stranger in town, a migrant and a German (Germans were driven out of the town after the First World War and the street names changed. Petersburg became Peterborough).

The Nursery

My prices were low, the stock was fresh and the customers had friendly service. When I couldn't answer their questions, I made a special effort to find out and get the stock they asked for. Through order sheets and inquiries, I soon learned a lot about plants and their names.

Gradually, I became quite busy. I needed help for cleaning my apartment and watering my garden—the rent agreement for my house did not include the garden. I talked to Lois, one of my happiest customers, who had become a friend of mine, about it. She offered to do both.

It was still a long working day beginning from 5am, sometimes lasting to midnight. The book-keeping and placing orders at night was made very pleasant though with a glass of champagne. The orders always came back with a lot of colour and variety.

The work didn't stop me either from making time to look after the place of my artist friend, Annette, during her exhibition in Melbourne, after hours. Annette was running a hotel in a previous convent in Peterborough and kept horses, geese, cats, and more on this property. I was rewarded with two of her paintings.

My social life had improved considerably with birthday parties and BBQs with friends from the garden club, horticulture centre, and nursery.

The nursery had to be expanded with more stands to raise more seedlings. Friends helped out with bases of beds, which were perfect because they had ventilation, but they were a bit low. The variety of stock increased also with special sales of fruit trees, cyclamens, and orchids. I formed an orchid club. Sections for statues and blacksmith work were added. I was changing the gardens of the town and the interest in gardening of the citizens.

Unfortunately, I had two break-ins with stock stolen and statues damaged. I was not insured because it would have been too expensive for the open area. It wasn't too bad though. Things returned to normal quickly after I installed security lights, but then another danger struck—a locust plague heading straight towards Peterborough. Someone up there looked after me. Two kilometres from the town the wind changed and the locusts went south. My open nursery had been saved.

I allowed myself the luxury of investing in an automatic irrigation system in my garden. It worked famously. A new electric stove (I didn't like my gas stove) and hot water service were also welcome achievements.

Towards the end of 1999, the success in my business started to claim a price. As I received more and more deliveries, my back started to play up. I paid Lois one of my best customers and good friend to help me to unload the cartons and place the plants in their spots. That became uneconomical. I couldn't raise the prices too much without losing customers. The doctor sent me for x-rays and it was established that I had a compressed vertebra. I was booked in a hospital for cortisone injections. They were extremely painful and effective only for four weeks. The situation made me think of selling the nursery. I talked to my lovely helper, Lois, about this and she immediately wanted to buy it. It was still a hard decision. I was very happy with what I was doing and could not imagine living without the nursery. It gave me purpose in life.

We organised a stocktaking sale in December. I did the painstaking count alone.

We needed a lawyer to get the papers done for the sale of the *Little Garden Centre* for the end of January 2000. Settlement would be in February. That meant I unwillingly retired at 65. Everything worked out perfectly with the rent agreement for my house, where in the last year a nursing sister with her two lovely, well-behaved daughters had lived. I was extremely lucky with my tenants.

My net profit from the sale was $3,800 (nineteen times the investment). The business provided me with an excellent lifestyle made me many friends, and allowed for some investments in my home and garden. It also landed me into trouble with four proposals! One came from my next-door neighbour and three from customers. One was an alcoholic, another fifteen years my senior, a fanatical member of the RSL who glorified war, clashing with my views as a peace worker. When I turned him down he sold his house and moved into a RSL retirement village, a much better solution for him. He said he could not live in the same town where I lived. The third had too many secrets, he was hiding something.

The last one, I took seriously. He was a retired Qantas pilot with a vast range of interests and talents. The day after he proposed to me, after we spent a wonderful day talking and celebrating our first private get-together, he planned a trip to Melbourne to attend his daughter's wedding. He was killed in an accident with a truck, which turned from the left lane beside him to the right just in front of him. When he didn't return a week later, as planned, I went to see him at his place and found a 'For Sale' sign on it. I only learned the news from the real estate agent. It was a great shock. It looked like I wasn't meant to be married. I was home alone again.

It didn't take long and I had new plans. I attended computer courses at TAFE and also did a course called 'assignments by choice' with the opportunity for public speaking about the assignments. I chose a number of issues—justice, mind, soul, and spirit, question belief, and Iraq at war. It was challenging work.

Besides that, I started to dig out a pond. I planned a large pond with plants and gold fish. The digging was hard going. I was sitting on limestone and needed a crowbar. After many slow attempts, I finished a hole two by four meters with a step for plants of different heights. My nephew, Ralph, the second son of my sister, came to my rescue and cemented the hole, which gave cause for celebration.

Not much later I bought a kit for a shade house. I was lucky again. This time two nephews, Ralph and his brother, Stephen, who were on holiday, helped me. The shade house was erected in no time. Another celebration followed.

Top: View to the Shade house, below: The Pond

A few weeks later, I experienced severe chest pains and went for a check-up at the surgery. I collapsed just after arriving and was seen by the doctor immediately. He checked my heart. It was alright. Then he checked side effects of lithium and there it was—chest pain was a side effect. I took my medication religiously. By that time I was without a bipolar episode for nine years. We both felt sure I was okay. The doctor took me off lithium within a fortnight without replacing it with another medication.

Within a month I started hallucinating. I was possessed by the idea that we were at war and went to tell the policeman who lived next door. He sent me home, where I started to play loud music, startling a neighbour who complained to the police. The policeman took me to the hospital from where I was transferred to Adelaide's Howard House—a hospital for older people. It was a dark, dirty place, and they put me back on lithium. As usual, when I was admitted to a hospital, my first thought was, *I have to get out of there*. It took me five weeks to convince the staff that I was well enough to go home.

It was not easy to fit in again. People shunned me. My secret was out. Now they didn't want to know me.

My nursery had changed hands again. Lois had too much car trouble and couldn't meet the bills. The new owner was a friend of mine from the horticulture centre. She took me in as an assistant for casual work. That showed people I was still human and gradually some became friendlier again.

After regaining some of my confidence, I had another plan. I wanted to add a back veranda to my house. I discussed this with Ralph, as he is a builder. He offered to make the plan, get the material, and build it. Not long after that he had a break from his contract work and came with his wife, Dawn, to stay at my place and the three of us went to work.

Ralph did all the measuring and building while Dawn and I were the labourers. Beside that I did the cooking.

It was hard work but the veranda quickly took shape and gave the house a welcoming look. It was a pleasure to see Ralph's speedy and accurate accomplishment. After a few days, the house was transformed. It made such a difference. I was so proud of my helpers.

There was soon something else I wanted changed to feel really comfortable in my home. In the last two years, I noticed salt damp appearing in several places in and outside the house. I asked for quotes from two companies for repairs. They were far out of my reach. Again, Ralph came to my rescue in the year 2003. He gave me a quote, far below than the other builders. I went to the bank and arranged a loan. This was the biggest venture on my place yet.

Ralph and Dawn came with their caravan and stayed till it was done. The encasing of the front veranda had to be pulled down and replaced. The walls in the hall and outside the bathroom needed repair and repainting. It was a very dusty undertaking and a big clean-up of the whole house was needed. It was more expensive than we first thought because there was so much to do, but I could pay the balance off in three months. What a wonderful supporter Ralph was. I fully enjoyed my house now and thought it would be my paradise for the rest of my life.

Unexpectedly, a few months later, my health began to play up. Arthritis pain in my knees joined my back problems and this complicated my life.

After several more months, the pain had become so severe that bending, kneeling, and getting up off the knees was only possible with the support of branches of trees in the garden and cupboards in the house. Walking up steps and getting in and out of cars or buses was also a problem. It became so bad that the doctor suggested a wheelchair for me. Medication was out of the question because I was allergic to painkillers. I was horrified. That was not the life I had imagined for me.

I began to think of moving back to Adelaide. I was sure I would get other help there.

I put my house on the market in the year 2004, a heartbreaking decision. It took a few months and two agents to find a buyer, in spite of all the improvements.

With the support of my son I found a unit near two hospitals, the Repatriation and Flinders hospitals. Then the inevitable had to be done. I had to organise a big garage sale. There were many things I had to get rid of because there was not enough space in the unit—no shed and only a very small garden. I could not have handled a big garden. The sale gave me a good return but I wondered whether I would miss things in the future.

I was lucky. I sold nearly everything. Some of it went to the buyer of the house and the rest to locals. What remained was taken by the second-hand shop. The owner of that shop handled my move to Adelaide. I was allowed to travel in the truck, like I did on the way up. We had a good trip. I was sure I had made the right decision. My health was the first priority.

RETURN TO ADELAIDE

Moving into the small unit met with some challenges. My five-seater couch and the six-seater dining setting proved to be too big to fit in. Further decisions were necessary. The furniture proved to be hard to sell. So I gave the dining setting to the Salvation Army and the couch to my son. I needed smaller items for replacement. I bought a Swedish ivory leather couch and a four-seater dining setting. Then the unit became quite comfortable.

Now I could attend to my health issues. In the Repatriation hospital, my teeth, which had been badly looked after in Peterborough, were treated and adjusted and in the Flinders hospital I received physiotherapy and hydrotherapy for my arthritis. The arthritis treatment helped only temporarily. The treatment in the Flinders hospital took six months, without a lasting effect. The same applied for treatment with massage and acupuncture from a naturopath. The doctors in Flinders recommended moving to the beach and swimming in saltwater. That was the only solution they had hopes for.

There was another development at that time. I had a very good general practitioner. She sent me to several specialists for thorough check-ups. A private psychiatrist was one of them. I convinced her that I had to come off lithium to be able to think clearly again and use my memory, especially as far as my education was concerned. She agreed that a change of medication was called for after such a long time on lithium (twenty-seven years) and put me on epilim (or valproate). The change was taken very slowly with reducing lithium and gradually increasing the new medication till it reached the required level. I was beginning to feel so much better with myself and started to think creatively again.

The treatments in hospitals and from the naturopath reduced my savings. To buy a house in Adelaide was out of the question. I was not able to raise the necessary mortgage on the pension. I began looking for a place to rent near the beach.

I also enrolled in a correspondence course 'Abundance for life' with Learning Strategies in Minnesota. The course was about setting goals and achieving them. I had to choose seven goals. My first goal was a house near the beach (listing details of colours of the house and the size of the garden). The second goal was getting the finance for it. The next one was achieving happiness and further more personal goals.

To my surprise, I found a place of my description in Aldinga Beach. I focused on Aldinga Beach because it was an area I was familiar with, which was not far from where our winery used to be. The rent was just affordable. The inspection disclosed a newly refurbished house with my favourite colours, a stainless steel stove, and polished floors, but it was even smaller than the unit I was in.

Improvements were a tank and a shed in the backyard. The front yard needed clearing. Thistles were over two feet high. The lawn in the back wanted a good haircut, too. The closeness to the beach (two minutes' walk) won me over. I signed the tenancy agreement and prayed that the furniture would fit in.

Another move had to be organised. I collected cartons from a factory and began packing. I had become quite experienced in that now. The removalist (I had two quotes) charged as much as the removalist from Peterborough to Adelaide (a trip of 250 km), but everything reached the new place in good condition. I marked everything with the name of the room which made the shifting easy. The furniture did fit. It was good to have a shed.

A few days after my move, my son came to help with the garden. I found a contractor to cut the lawn as I had no mower. We cleared the thistles and heaped them up for the rubbish truck.

Robbie was still there when I felt one night I was sinking . . . sinking . . .

sinking instead of falling asleep. He took me to Flinders hospital. After a long waiting time they transferred me to the Repatriation hospital. I had a relapse into bipolar psychosis. I stayed there for five weeks. Doctors told me the episode could have been caused because I felt totally lost. I knew nobody, I had no connections, I did not even know how to get to the shopping centre. The loss of my home and the change of medication could also have played a role.

When I left the hospital they assigned a nurse from an organisation of the Catholic Church to me to help me get into the community. She was very helpful and gave me a contact to the community centre, where I joined the 'Friendship Club'. I met a German lady there and other friendly members. The program was enjoyable with speakers on different topics, outings to reserves and luncheons. I made two speeches in the community centre during the multicultural term—Germany today and Christmas in Germany. I was well received. Nobody knew about my stage fright.

After a few months, the program became repetitive and I began looking for something new. I found the Coastal Capers. They had speakers, too, and regular afternoon tea in the café in the shopping centre. Even that became boring. I needed something challenging like TAFE had been in Peterborough.

I met my dear friend, Betty, from the winery unexpectedly in the shopping centre. I was very fortunate to still have this wonderful friend after forty years. We always kept in contact. It was wonderful to be with someone who knew me better than anybody and stuck to me in spite of my illness. Betty introduced me to the library, where I became a regular visitor. We did several outings for lunch or afternoon tea together and went to op shops.

These outings reduced my budget to a hardly sustainable level. I went to the Housing Trust and tried to hurry my position in the queue. It was no use. I was told, I had to wait twenty years for a place unless I wanted to move into a one bedroom cabin. I wasn't prepared for that, but they gave me the connection to Co-Op Housing organisations.

I contacted the head office SASHA of these organisations and was given a kit of information for this style of living. I had to pass an ICH course (Information Course for Community Housing). The organisations were actually private corporations, subsidised by the government. They only charged 25% of the income for rent, which would greatly improve my budget.

I passed the course, which was really quite complicated with a lot of legislation to be learned. At the end of the course, the teacher, a tenant of a Co-Op Housing Corporation Inc., told me her organisation had four vacancies. I applied the next day. By the time they were ready for an interview in December of that year, the vacancies were gone. However, they needed a maintenance manager. I applied for the position and was accepted because of my experience in my three businesses.

Another house became available in February 2007. My first impression was not very good. It was a cottage style house in the established part of Aldinga Beach. When I had a look inside though, I was rapt. It was fully-carpeted, had large rooms—especially the lounge, dining area, and kitchen with its lots of built-in cupboards. The bathroom and laundry were also a good size. A bonus was the high ceilings. I could breathe! Everything was solid, better than in the new homes. There was so much room that I could add some furniture.

The place was a few minutes further away from the beach, but close to the shopping centre and the library. The bus stop was two minutes away. The Aldinga scrub and the wetlands were fifteen minutes away and everything was surrounded by vineyards. The hills lined the southern border of the district. I couldn't ask for a better position. To be able to move, I had to find a tenant for my unit to get out of the contract. I was lucky. I found someone within three weeks.

Another move! Hopefully, that would be the last one.

Just before I moved, I struck up a conversation with the new tenant of the unit about religion. She seemed to share a lot of my beliefs, especially about the future including events leading up to the year 2012. She invited me to her church, which happened to be the Revival Fellowship. It awakened many memories about my experiences with religions.

RELIGION IN MY LIFE

- -

I was christened and had my confirmation in the Lutheran Church. Our family was not very religious. Our visits to the church were limited to Christmas. I was not impressed by our church.

When I was in college, I found friendships with two classmates who were curious about religions. We visited a class of converts in the Catholic Church. I withdrew very soon because of the teachings that babies and children dying without christening would not go to heaven in spite of not having sinned in this world. My friends converted to the Catholic Church. One became a priest later and the other became a nun.

Religion didn't play an important role in my life until I suffered from bipolar. I was searching for answers. I needed a connection to a higher power, which could give me the answer to 'why me?' and 'what is the meaning of this?'

I mentioned before how I made contact with the Church of Jesus Christ of Latter Days Saints (the Mormons) when I played the songs of the Mormon Tabernacle Choir and the missionaries came to the door. The second time they contacted me I was baptised after a short membership. A few members of the church celebrated with me, sitting on the floor drinking fruit juice and nibbling cakes and biscuits.

I went to two of their chapels and became actively involved in their excellent educational programs. In their teachings the story of Josef Schmidt left the deepest impression on me, especially when the Lord appeared to him as light and told him about the golden plates. I developed a longing desire to see God like that.

The Elders made an attempt to heal me from bipolar but were unsuccessful. They decided I wasn't humble enough. They still made me a missionary, but soon called me from my post because I didn't believe in the devil. I believe God has given us choices. When we make the wrong choices, it is our fault. There is no devil involved.

They also made the statement that my son is a devil because he was misbehaving badly at that time. The church didn't have the right to make that judgment about anybody. Robert had a hard time adjusting to the fact that he was adopted and that I had divorced Gabor and he had become a rebel since. Unfortunately, Gabor let him have his way too much. I left the church soon after that.

Not much later, I was confronted by two members of the Church of Scientology, who promised after a long conversation to cure me from bipolar. I wanted nothing more than that and was quite vulnerable because of it. I followed them to the head office, was interviewed by a member of the staff with a lie detector, bought the book *Dianetics* and enrolled in an information course.

The course was based on the book and turned out to be the preparation for the work they do for people with traumas and mentally ill people. I found the course very interesting. I learned how to express my feelings or a story in clay and to find the real meaning of a word in dictionaries. It needed sometimes more than one dictionary, especially with different languages. I was fascinated by the simple method used for erasing traumas and thereby healing people. The client is put into a relaxed state of mind, similar to hypnosis, by counting and then following their memory lane, clearing traumas by repetition till the trauma is forgotten. I wanted that applied to me but was refused treatment because I was on medication and would not give it up. They let me finish the training and even gave me clients—only 'cleared' people were allowed to 'clear' others by the rules of Scientology.

My first client was from Finland. She had a wonderful upbringing, a lovely family, and a safe, rich lifestyle. I couldn't do anything for her. It was a different story with the second client. He was obviously under the influence of drugs, and by the rules of Scientology, should not be allowed for a clearing. I ignored all that and prepared for a treatment. He was reminded to tell only the truth. I had the feeling he was very insecure, but we moved through some small traumas very quickly, but then he got his memory right back into the womb. I thought he was lying and stopped the session to ask for advice from the head office. They assured me that this experience is quite possible and asked me to go back and continue the session.

On returning to my client, we started to pick up his last memory. He told me how he was moving around in the womb and how he heard his parents speaking about the baby (him) always referring to it as a girl. When he was born the doctor announced, 'it's a boy!'

I felt that this was where the problem lay. His insecurity seemed to have stemmed from the fact that he wasn't sure whether he was a girl or a boy. I made him repeat 'it's a boy' dozens of times. It finally sank in and he relaxed. I closed the session and he jumped up in the happiest mood, ran to the head office, and told everyone he had never been happier in his life. The staff celebrated with me and someone said, 'you are one of the most powerful people in the world'. I wasn't sure where that came from but gathered that it must have been because I had cleared someone (in one session), me being on medication and the patient on drugs. That was not normal procedure in the church.

I left the church soon after that because they seemed to drag the clearing (healing) out by only dealing with one trauma at the time and then postponing for further sessions to make more money. For me, that was using people who are most vulnerable and in need of help. Apart from that, they went into my account (they had the details) for payments for a set of speeches from Ron Hubbard, which I didn't order. I felt betrayed and wanted to resign from the church, which proved very difficult. I had to go through several interviews and was tested with a lie detector. I called on Consumer Affairs for help to get me out of there. I received very helpful advice and was released from the church.

I found deeper insight in religious beliefs during discussions with my friend, Robert, whom I met during my first hospital stay. We studied a number of religions in the search of a better connection to God. After Christianity, Indian religions captured our interests, including Buddhism, Hinduism, and Taoism.

We also studied Islam and Judaism. Robert had a vast collection of books with scriptures, comments, and practices. He read to me and we discussed the contents for fourteen years till we both moved. I moved to Peterborough and Ian to Queensland. We also visited the Assembly of God several times, but neither of us committed to any of these religions. We were still searching for the right faith. There is the same God in all religions. There really should be only one church. They all have good intentions but each of them claims they are the only right one. That's why there are always religious wars.

I did some research with Hare Krishna's followers, who taught me about reincarnation and enlightened me that bipolar is the result of negative and materialistic thinking. By their beliefs, materialistic thinking reaches as far as possessiveness of loved ones when someone dies and people grieve because they are sorry for themselves. They do not grieve when they believe in reincarnation. This was an amazing opening for me. I believed they were right, but it didn't cure me.

Apart from these studies, I contacted a group of the Brahma Kumaris' faith and wanted to visit their temple in the Himalaya. They wanted me to work as a missionary in Peterborough but I declined because I had no training.

In Peterborough, I had little involvement with religion. I attended the Seventh-Day Adventists for a short while but got in trouble again with them with my beliefs about the devil. They did give me vast information about a number of religions for an assignment at TAFE.

All these previous experiences came back to me when I was invited to the Revival Fellowship in Aldinga. I visited their church a few times and even was baptised (again!), but left them when they expected me to go door-knocking with them to spread their beliefs. That was too much for me. I believed people should find their faith with their own experiences, not by being talked into it at the door. Very few respond anyway. That was my last experience with a church. I did not find a connection to God in any of them.

But then came an answer to my needs. One day, I heard about the U3A—University of the third age—an international organisation with a wide range of interests. By chance I met the secretary of the group in the library and a new chapter in my life began.

HAPPINESS WITH THE U3A

- -

The U3A started in France in 1972 and became international in 1975. It gained recognition by the UN and UNESCO. The Aldinga Group was founded in January 1997 with forty-eight members and five different courses. It was linked to Adelaide's universities and now has up to thirty courses and activities.

I joined in 2005. The program, headed by the logo of an owl, addressed several of my interests—history, music, literature, poetry, theatre, computing, philosophy, discussion groups, a lecture series, films, walking and cycling groups, senior adventurers, luncheon club, and social activities.

I chose four groups for the first term—philosophy, discussion, walking and adventurers, and attended the lectures of Adelaide's universities. There were about two hundred members in the organisation, many names to learn. Most groups had about twenty participants and a wonderful relaxed and friendly atmosphere. I felt fully accepted and even though I was probably the poorest member of the U3A; I was treated equally, which gave me my confidence back. I felt, after many years, I belonged somewhere and began to enjoy my freedom and the company of the different groups.

Aldinga is a place where intellectuals retire. I was among business people, lecturers, artists, and writers—much like the customers of our winery, who I missed for a long time. There was never a lack of an interesting discussion topic. Anybody had the chance to participate in learning, teaching, planning and administration, and join any or all groups.

I started in the walking group. We met at the library and had a car pool, which was fortunate for me since I had no car. We drove to certain places and walked from there. This way we were able to see our beautiful surroundings. Members of the group were teaching me the history, function, and significance of places and I also learned a lot about the fauna and flora of the region.

We had fabulous views along walks on top of the hills and took great pleasure strolling through scrubs, forests, and along the beach. I never had the opportunity of discovering the surroundings when I lived in the district before because of my busy involvement with the winery. There was very little time for outings except swimming at the beach. Now we were walking once a week for two hours. After the walks we visited the tempting bakery on our way. I took up photography to capture the memories and gradually became the photographer of the U3A. Through members of the walking group, I made contact with the senior adventurers—a very enterprising group with many different ideas and interests.

The adventurers of the U3A had a meeting once a month to plan a program and discuss events. The program was very colourful. Beside the program for the month there was consideration given to future events. The list could take up to thirty suggestions such as:

A trip to Kangaroo Island
Camping and fishing at Rapid Bay

Mystery car tours (some of my favourites)

Cable hang gliding, Aldinga flights

Hot air ballooning, adventure trails

Day trips exploring Adelaide's hills areas

Exhibitions, archery

Exploring historic buildings in Mildura and Clare

Visiting Murray lands or Mallee Country

Travelling to Melbourne on the Great Ocean Road—visiting markets and Ballarat

National parks and reserves

Ten-day trip through the outback

Ten pin bowling, yearly crab feast

Mannum trip, houseboat tour

Festival in Alice Springs, Port Adelaide dolphin tour and much more.

We never ran out of ideas.

I didn't participate in all of the events, but had a wonderful time on many short trips. I did a lot of things I'd never done before, having the most memorable experiences.

The tour in the outback in October 2006 was the highlight of it all. We did car-pooling, as always, and travelled with five vehicles (three camper vans) and twelve people on a warm morning in high spirits bound for Roxby Downs and beyond. Our first stop was the caravan park at Spears Creek near Port Augusta, which was a working sheep station. We came across only a dozen sheep. There was hardly any stock anywhere. It was a drought year.

We camped under large eucalyptus trees in an old creek bed. The travellers without a car stayed in comfortable cabins. At night fall, we had a get-together, after we had a meal with our own food, and a drink under the cloud-free sky. In the morning we headed to Glendambo and had a lovely BBQ.

From Glendambo we went to Coober Pedy. It was a very hot day—forty five degrees in the shade and very strong northerly winds. We had planned a three-day stopover with an early start on the outback mail run for a twelve-hour trip to outlying stations, where we were warmly welcomed. Even in this prime cattle country where the best beef is grown on account of the dry fodder which gives special flavour to meat, we saw only one herd of cattle. After this tour we moved to Oodnadatta, an aboriginal town, down the Oodnadatta Track to Williams Creek. I took some photos of the well—decorated school, the museum, and of some aboriginal elders (with their permission). Then it was back to Coober Pedy.

We had free time the next morning and discovered what this unique town had to offer. It was not only opals! The underground buildings and mines were fascinating. The imagination of the adventurous miners was obvious in all their decorations and other expressions of art. We found the underground quarters of the Crocodile Hunter who mined a whole hill to make quarters for the aboriginals from Maralinga. The hunter was very old and tired. He died a few days after our visit, but left a treasure chest of souvenirs.

In the afternoon, we made a tour to the 'Moon planes', the field of shafts and open mines. Among them is the golf course where they use a small green square to hit the ball from. It was ingenious.

The last night we even watched an object moving in a strange way, which we believed could have been a UFO, while gathering for our usual get-together at night, after we had a fabulous prawn dinner in the Greek café. Fresh prawns in the middle of the desert! They told us they get fresh deliveries daily by plane.

The next morning, we travelled to Roxby Downs. On the way there, we paid a short visit to Woomera where we admired the Rocket Park and did get a brief glimpse of the Rocket Station, on my request. I wanted to see what it looked like after the Japanese took it over. We drove through the open gate with a STOP sign, but our leader made us turn around to avoid trouble, for which he would have blamed me. I was prepared for that. I thought by remembering names of US Air force officers, who invited us to the station, I would get away with it—even with Japanese.

Arriving in Roxby Downs, we toured the modern mining town and, after our guided tour of the Olympic dam was cancelled, we enjoyed a film about the workings in the mine with all the huge machines. Women were working there, too. It was very impressive.

From there we toured Andamooka, where we found some of the earliest buildings in Australia and attempted to find some opals—we did!—and also some seeds of Sturt desert peas. Then we returned to Roxby Downs for the night. The next morning it was back to Spears Creek where we celebrated our last night around a camp fire, making marshmallows and enjoyed the last home-cooked meal. We really grew together on this trip. The camaraderie was at all times on a high level. None of us will forget this trip.

I stayed with the group for three years until my arthritis got the better of me again and travelling was too strenuous. But I still want to do hot air ballooning and 'Aldinga flights'.

While I was attending the walking group once a week and the adventurers up to four times a month, I also took part in the philosophy group with a teacher from South Africa. It was a step into the unknown but because of my curiosity; I quickly grew into the vast offering of topics.

We met fortnightly and established a program at first for two terms and later for a whole year. Our teacher gave a talk for sixty to ninety minutes on most of the topics, but we had volunteers for some subjects.

I prepared myself for the lessons by researching the issues beforehand and was therefore able to participate in the discussions. I also read an anthology of western philosophy for certain topics.

The following issues were included in the 2005 program—knowledge, ethics, racism, anti-semitism, democracy, communism, liberalism, fascism, and immortality amongst others.

In 2006, we went into subjects like the mind, God and the problem of evil, religion and morality, the origin of the universe, evolution, memory, language, euthanasia, and life after death, spirituality, feminism, the just war and so on. In that year I made my first attempt for a talk about mind, soul, and spirit—a topic I presented at TAFE in Peterborough. I was quite nervous but was well-received.

The year 2007 brought further fascinating subjects like the nature of science, science and religion, genetic engineering, the meaning of life, reason, homophobia, consciousness, globalisation, previous life, and so on. I dared to give another talk that year speaking about creativity. I put the emphasis on human creativity and included a glimpse into nature's creativity, which is a vast subject and gives enough content for a separate talk. I received another good response.

While happily involved with the U3A, something happened in my private life that year. I ran into difficulties with the maintenance group of the Co-Op. The members of the group were totally inexperienced in management procedures, became afraid of my speed, and started backstabbing and undermining decisions made in the meetings. Since I couldn't run the group under these circumstances, I asked the president for a solution.

The management organised a special meeting in which they gave me two options—either I work alone or get a transfer to a Housing

Association—without any consideration of my own situation. I gladly accepted the second option, especially since they planned to sell the house to the association. This meant I didn't have to move. I knew I wouldn't have to work for an association as they employed professionals and I did not have to attend any meetings.

The transfer was arranged within a few weeks, after the acceptance of an association with very friendly personnel. I was extremely grateful for this turn of events. My home was secure as long as I paid the rent, which was arranged by payments through Centrelink. I felt free and at peace.

Year 2008 brought another interesting program for philosophy with subjects like the origin of religion, the soul, nature of time, happiness, inspiration, free will, censorship, humanism, the nature of family. I took up the challenge of prophecy and paranormal, which gave me plenty of themes to talk about. I received applause and thanks for that talk but also upset a few members with my open opinions about paranormal issues and my views on prophecies for the year 2012.

I left the group because I had become involved with Australian Cosmic Connection, which I will discuss later. This doesn't mean I lost interest in the U3A. It is my family since I have hardly any contact with my own family and nearly all my friends were in the U3A. I spent a short time with the discussion group, which was dealing with topics from the news or interesting issues like windmill farms, hot rock companies and the environment.

In another fascinating group we dealt with spirituality, discussing ethics, morality, religion versus spirituality, technology versus science and, of course, the definition of spirituality. In one term we learned about living in the NOW. When I noticed that members of the group did not apply what they learned, I started to look for other interests.

Because I love the atmosphere of theatres, I took over managing the theatre group when a vacancy of a leader occurred. Before the new season started, I had doubled the number of their membership, plus a few on standbys when someone was not able to use a ticket. I met a very special lady through this group—a ballet dancer from London— who danced *Giselle* several times. Part of the story of that ballet is like a big part of my own story. The ballet was the inspiration of my name *Giselle*. We also shared the same name (my middle name), which gave us a strong bond. However, I didn't stay long with that group either, because I didn't enjoy the plays in the Dunstan Theatre as they usually contained scenes with alcohol consumption and swearing. I sold my remaining tickets and found a new leader. The group is still going strong.

At different stages, I also visited the computing class. I am not very technically-minded but need the computer a lot for my email and research—my insatiable hobby. I had to compete with real experts but they were very patient with me and helped me sort out quite a few queries.

I didn't miss another very pleasant group, the luncheon club. The meetings were always happy but even so I didn't always enjoy the restaurant foods. I cook with herbs myself and find, when eating out, the food can be very boring, but the company (about twenty members) made up for it. We visited local hotels and restaurants on the beach and among the vineyards and always had a great time.

For weekends there was special entertainment by the weekend capers, mostly for single people but also for couples, which had their weekends free. We did day trips within shorter distances, had lunch on the way in Victor Harbor or river towns, and went to local theatres, garden festivals, and wineries. We appreciated each other's company while having interesting discussions about all sorts of news and interests. I had a problem staying with that group because of lack of transport. There was no regular car pool, but I had the chance to travel with others many times.

The most overwhelming occurrence in the U3A happened in the group 'show and tell' where we showed our treasures and explained the meaning of their importance to the participants. I showed a large framed photograph of a double exposure of a barn owl which won the first prize in a bird exhibition in the Adelaide Museum. It was a very impressive shot by a well-known photographer. I took two years to save up for it. Then a lady I hardly knew stood up and said she had a special treasure, too, and took out a bottle of our first release of our vintage port from the year 1975 and gave it to me! She knew my story from the winery. I was speechless. The wine is priceless! All I was able to do was give her a big hug and my own treasure—the owl. She happened to like owls, too.

Berenyi's Port - Vintage 1975

I am still following the lectures and film afternoons and may go back to other groups after I finalise some private interests. I had four days a week booked out for the U3A till the end of 2008, when I had some turbulent experiences. I found friends, knowledge and wisdom, adventure and wonderful new experiences in the U3A, which led to great happiness in my life and was the rescue from a purposeless existence.

In addition to my experiences in the U3A—driven by my never-ending thirst for knowledge about the universe—I found Australian Cosmic Connection, an organisation which followed Adelaide's UFO Club, which no longer existed after the leader retired.

ABUNDANCE WITH AUSTRALIAN COSMIC CONNECTION

Australian Cosmic Connection is a non-profit international organisation, which meets once a month. I was lucky that the leader of the group, Kevin Robb, offered to take me there since there was no public transport available for night-time meetings.

The meetings are public. There is no membership involved, but there are about two hundred listed contacts in South Australia, who used to be personally informed about the meetings. Now events are published on the internet. I have attended the meetings since 2006. The organisation was founded over ten years ago. It has the purpose of support for people with extra-terrestrial experiences and to educate the public on the higher realities of ultraterrestrial-extraterrestrial interventions with humankind. The aim is to inform the people that they have a choice with what energies they want to interact with for the greater good.

I heard that earlier on, there have been energies visiting the planet, which may not have had our highest interests at heart and abductions and slaughter of animals have occurred. Recently, a consciousness shift of humanity made people think more about love and the meaning of life than money. I believe we are seeing divine beings coming here to remind us who we really are.

The leader of our group sees his purpose in re-educating the mass population through mass healing workshops and lectures—creating guidance and direction to allow people to reach their full potential positively. He has a healing centre on Mount Magnificent, south of Adelaide, where a lot of sightings of UFOs and appearances of lights or energy centres (orbs) have occurred. The program of the meetings includes lectures and DVDs containing documentaries and DVDs about extra-terrestrial encounters, among those documentaries by James Gilliland (well-known from lectures and radio programs); UFO crashes (contact of extraterrestrials can be traced back by scriptures and inscriptions on rocks for thousands of years); secret UFO bases on the planet, secrecy of the governments; crop circles, which taught us to differentiate between real (created by air pressure) and human-made rolled circles; disappearance of ships (Bermuda Triangle), prophecies about coming changes of the planet, which will effect everyone of us and so on. DVDs on these topics are available for hire at the meetings.

The above-named topics don't fully cover the programs of the meetings. There were evenings when we handled subjects of naturalism such as remedies for alternative medicine, diet, exercise, effects of stress on the spirit, acupuncture, and massage. A tour through an organisation making organic healing products was also arranged.

Other topics include subjects from the paranormal, astronomy, astrology, out-of-body and near-death experiences and an introduction to the consciousness development program. Highlights of the year were presented by the adventurer, explorer, writer and photographer, Rex Gilroy, who covered Australia's pre-history with stories about settlers and miners from the copper and bronze ages with findings of pyramids, lost cities and settlements, Celtic ruins and inscriptions—all covered with samples and photographs (some including orbs) to prove it.

Gilroy found traces of early settlers like Egyptians, Phoenicians, Asians, Norwegians, and Spanish. The Europeans from England and other countries were only recent additions. He also found traces of giants, a yowie, and a net of tunnels under the surface of the continent. Rex also lifted the veil of the secret underground Australian/American bases and the ET connection in the Blue Mountains.

Gilroy's findings created controversy with the universities. I found his book *Mysterious Australia*, compelling reading.

Other highlights in Cosmic Connection are the weekend camping tours to the Flinders, Waitpinga Beach, and Mount Magnificent with meditation, chanting, music with drums and other instruments. A night watch, usually with sightings of UFOs and orbs, often takes place.

By getting news from national and international resources including NASA, UFO Queensland and through the close connection with Sacred Resonance, Cosmic Connection is always disseminating the newest information.

Darren Curtis and Bradley Pitt, the founders of Sacred Resonance, gave regular presentations with talks and DVDs added greatly to the colourful program of Cosmic Connection. Sacred Resonance is a non-profit membership organisation. They have developed advanced meditation, healing and consciousness, creating CDs and DVDs based on Darren's research in universities, with honours from Adelaide University in sound healing, and direct experience with leading spiritual thinkers and composers around the world, fusing frequency patterns found in nature and supernature, also advanced sound patterns found within all major pyramids of the world.

This music expresses the perfection of creation, allowing us to have direct consciousness experiences. Higher intelligence has guided their work and research in areas as extensive as sacred sonics, quantum physics, archeoastronomy, cosmology, UFOlogy and sacred visual art. They show how spirituality merges with nature and supernature.

Their use of geometric forms especially pyramids, describing the growth and integration of all systems within atoms to the shape and composition of galaxies presented in the images on DVDs captured my special interest as I like mathematics. The combination with an expressive colour scheme makes such a presentation unforgettable. The DVDs ancient lands, Spectra—journey to hyperspace and Nadaum were the first ones I bought, but there are many more on the market now.

In their own workshops, Darren and Bradley discuss the planets and solar system, celestial sphere, the universe and beyond, how we can initiate contact with cosmic evolutions, the world energy grid, the truth behind the light veil and much more. I also attended a talk show in the planetarium (where they work regularly) about 'spaceship earth' and was overwhelmed by the images, colours, and especially the sound effects. The presentation made me feel that we were travelling through the universe from galaxy to galaxy.

Darren and Bradley work closely with the Academy for Future Science in Los Gatos, USA. The Academy for Future Science is a non-profit corporation that examines new scientific ideas for the future. The principal goal of the academy is to provide all people with educational and scientific tools to help them meet the major transformation in social, cultural, economic, and emotional dimensions. Darren and Bradley introduced us to the book *The Keys of Enoch* by Dr J J Hurtak, the founder of the academy. Another book *Consciousness, Energy and Future Science* has a vast outlook into the future in the fields of archaeology, biology, environment, future science (chemistry and physics) and consciousness.

The academy has published an extensive collection of books, booklets, videos and DVDs, and runs a study program. Students without university background find the studies laborious but very rewarding. It is the highest education I have ever attempted. We saw a DVD in Cosmic Connection, which gave us an introduction to Dr J J Hurtak's work. He is a modest man and lives in spartan conditions.

As these pages show, there is no end of receiving knowledge through Cosmic Connection and their worldwide connecting organisations. I enjoyed the abundant programs as much as the company of the participants, who all had a story to tell. Abundance of life is everywhere but with Cosmic Connection it has a direction to eternity.

Through the activities with these groups, I lead a generally peaceful and happy life for four years. Events in 2008 changed all that.

EVENTFUL YEARS

- -

The year 2008 started with my dedication to grow trees for our district with *Trees for Life*, and the *Friends of the Scrub*. I propagated native plants and sold them to a hardware store. I also grew some vine cuttings for a friend who had bought my vines in Peterborough. Propagating plants was wonderful, restful, and creative work. My backyard coped admirably.

My godson and nephew, Manfred, his wife Zai (a Malaysian), and their youngest son, Mathew were surprise visitors from Melbourne. We spent a very special week together enjoying the beaches and eating out. Manfred raised a long-held wish to find his father, who had no contact with him since his mother, my sister, divorced him. I promised to look for him since I felt sure he was still living in South Australia.

A few weeks later, I went to the Electoral Office and I found his address. I notified Manfred and the family came back the next month to visit his father. It was a happy reunion and I was introduced to him, too, although I wasn't very keen to meet him because of earlier memories. But we all got along splendidly and I was invited for a holiday on Manfred's farm in Melbourne, at a time when he was on holiday from the oil rig. I was delighted since I missed living on the land, in spite of being happy where I was. I had everything I needed.

After Manfred and his family left, my thoughts went to Peterborough again. We experienced a year of bad droughts and I feared farmers could lose their land. I lost two farms and know what that means. The water supply in Peterborough was not secured. They had no storm water system and totally relied on Murray water from Adelaide. The Murray was running low.

I made contact with Greening Australia and received charts for rainfall and lists of plants and trees for drought areas. I organised a lecturer from Adelaide University, who could conduct a course for farmers on the issue. I took my findings to Peterborough where I discussed the issues with the mayor and director of TAFE and also made suggestions for a storm water system. The mayor presented me with a green and gold scarf with the words 'For the green lady of Peterborough' and we celebrated with a lovely dinner in her favourite hotel.

It wasn't only Peterborough I was concerned about. The state government planned a desalination plant in our district, in the Gulf St Vincent. I was totally opposed to it because the plan was to return the brine back into the sea. The gulf in our area has little flushing action. The heavy brine would sink to the sea floor and kill all marine life, which would change the health of the gulf. The citizens around it would be affected and, of course, the whole living style on the beaches and their attraction would deteriorate.

There is a market for salt and minerals, which can be extracted from the brine by catalysts. I found the US patents for that in my research and sent them to government officials. I started correspondence with the Water, Environment, and Health Ministers, the premier Mr Rann and the mayor for our district. I attended two forums conducted by the mayor and Adelaide's universities. I finally gave up writing to politicians because the government was only listening to advice from experts who agreed with them. They didn't take any notice of scientifically well-proven warnings about the project by professors from universities. Why should they listen to me or the public?

It wasn't quite the end of my campaign. A friend of mine put me in contact with Ruth Trigg. I read about her when the River Lakes and Coorong Action Group she belonged to stopped a weir being built across the River Murray, and when she and others strongly protested about a series of regulators being built to stop the flow of rivers into the Murray.

Ruth carried out vigils at the beach front of our district with some volunteers and I joined them. We wanted people to be aware of what would happen to our Gulf St Vincent if the desalination plant went ahead as planned. It is amazing how little people know about the works of nature and how cooperative they become when they learn about it.

Ruth has a deep love for the environment and an inestimable understanding of nature. She takes anybody on who wants to interfere with it and perseveres till she gets results. Her knowledge in law and government procedures makes her quite a formidable opponent for people who make decisions in these fields without the necessary knowledge of what it will involve. It is very inspiring to work with her.

Something completely different happened during this time. I learned that a German friend of mine from the U3A wanted to get rid of his German books because nobody in the family spoke German. I asked him if I could have them because my books were bequeathed to the state library and it would be a shame when his valuable books about explorers, adventurers, archaeologists, nature, and Olympics could be lost. He brought thirty of them to my place and made me buy a new bookshelf. It was fascinating reading. I was especially captured by stories from ancient countries and prehistory and Indian cultures.

I booked my trip to Melbourne to visit Manfred. We had a wonderful drive to their farm in a beautiful country setting. I had waited a few years for this opportunity but Manfred had rebuilt his three levels home from scratch and wanted it finished before he had any visitors.

It was an impressive building on top of a hill with a garden, wide lawns, and cattle yards around it. A tree-lined driveway led to the house. We drove into the garage in the basement of the house with an adjacent office. We climbed the stairs to the kitchen on the top level, joining the dining area and TV room on the next level. The kitchen had beautiful dark timber built-ins with a pantry and a huge stainless steel stove. We picked up a massive snapper and some ingredients at the market on the way home and started a Malaysian cooking session. I unpacked in 'my' room, where a remarkable bunch of purple orchids greeted me. There were three windows arranged in a half circle. I could almost overlook the whole farm and later watched beautiful sunrises.

Cooking together was great fun. The smells of Malaysian herbs and spices were delicious and the way of preparation a new cooking experience. Zai and I worked harmoniously together and the dinner became a feast.

The next day Manfred introduced me to the farm, the garden and the shade house with an incredible number of orchids—in need of help— and other plants. The shade house was heavily overcrowded and asking for attention. I felt very tempted to lend a hand. That doesn't mean that I didn't admire the cattle—a strong healthy herd—obviously very tame. The pasture was good and a dam was in the making from a small creek running through the property. The whole place was surrounded by trees and scrub.

Turning inside again for lunch, we discussed plans for the next days. My ambition to get stuck into the garden and shade house was greatly appreciated. I finally was able to use my surplus energy somewhere useful. I needed potting soil to firstly repot the orchids which were to be placed in the sun room. Manfred organised the soil and pots. The next day was filled with sorting and replanting the orchids, everyone helped and we soon accomplished the task—around thirty pots.

The next thing was weeding the other pots and reorganising the shade house. It was with great satisfaction when we viewed the final result after removing the weeds and the leaves. I was in my element.

Next morning, I planted potatoes and weeded the garden with help and supervision from Zai. It was a pretty tough job. There was a lot of buffalo grass mixing with the plants but we finished it and relaxed.

The following day, I had a new adventure. I was allowed to ride the sit-on mower. It was easy to handle. Even so, I was cautious because I ran it on a hillside. The result looked professional.

That night, some of the cattle were to go to the market. I had no idea how successful I could be in rounding them up. I had never done that before, but it worked. I had a very determined strong voice and they followed my direction. The loading was mostly Manfred's responsibility. He knew how they had to move on the trailer and after handling a few resistant cattle they were finally loaded.

We went to the market without problems. Manfred was allotted a pen for them and we drove in. The noise and the smell made me feel back in the country. After the paper work was done, Manfred went ahead and the agent said to me, 'just follow your husband'. We had a good laugh and went home safely.

A big surprise awaited me the next day. Manfred invited me for a ride on his motorbike. I was thrilled. I like motorbikes and his was a beauty. Wearing Manfred's boots, windcheater, and helmet I had an unforgettable ride through beautiful country roads at150km/h.

My remaining holiday was filled with helping with the clearing of overhanging branches on the driveway. Manfred did the cutting and I was feeding the cattle with the branches. The driveway when finished was very neat.

We celebrated Mothers Day with coffee and cake on the lawn and had a luxurious dinner in an Italian restaurant with the whole family, including their two sons, Michael and Mathew. On another day I watched Manfred digging the dam with a big bulldozer and front-end loader. I enjoyed spending time in the kitchen with Zai to do more creative cooking with her.

We spent a day shopping at the markets, a wonderful experience. I bought a good luck gem for Zai's birthday and a black Italian cardigan for myself. We enjoyed the bright colours, lights and goods in Chinatown which were especially impressive. I found a lovely tea set for a friend of mine at home.

After this excitement going home was a sad affair. It was the best holiday I had ever had with my family beside the holiday in Hamburg in 1992. I lived a life on this holiday I had wanted for a lifetime.

Returning home, I felt happy and contented. In this refreshed state I felt inspired. I wanted to write my autobiography and started research on World War II. I collected my records of hospital admissions with bipolar through the freedom of information act. I began writing in August 2008 and contacted a publisher.

To be able to get around a bit faster, to have more time available, I bought myself a mountain bike. I never got the full command over the brakes and had a bad fall when I had to brake hard on a T-junction when a number of cars approached suddenly from the left. It took me a while to get up—there was no help. I had severe back pain, but I went back on the bike and finished my trip to the garden store. I didn't go back on the bike after that as I had still trouble with my back. In spite of that I booked a trip to the outback with the outback pilot, Dick Lang. I love the outback and that year Lake Eyre was filled with water. This would make it a very special trip.

Amongst this excitement I received an email from a barrister in London who informed me that I was eligible for an inheritance of millions of dollars from a Robin's family who were killed in a car crash and had no heirs. The barrister had been notified by the bank to find any member of the extended family to put up a claim for the inheritance, which was in a term deposit in a bank, or the funds would be liquidated and made unserviceable in accordance with existing laws because it would be assumed that no member of the family was alive. He proposed a deal that fifty per cent of the net sum would be accrued to me at conclusion of the transfer.

Even though I was not a member of the family (I adopted my name) I agreed to the deal as I had two predictions by psychics that I would come into a lot of money and I wouldn't hurt anybody by accepting this arrangement. The barrister also advised me that Mr Robin was an independent oil magnate and his oil company had made moves to divert the funds in their interests and use the excuse that he was not able to find someone to make the claim. They wanted the money to be unserviceable, which means reverting the money to the government and then the company would get a percentage. This convinced me even more to accept the deal.

The barrister faxed me the documents of the term deposit and the contract for our arrangement (letter of guarantee) and an authority (including my IDs) to sign for another barrister, appointed by the bank, to get the transfer of the term deposit with the title office and the bank organised. I paid £4,250 for the transfer and £2,347 for completion of the job with the bank. The bank sent me a notification that my application has been approved and a congratulation for the activation of my account, but I was asked to pay 0.48% of the sum in question— namely £174,853 as transfer fees for the sum of thirty million pounds plus interests to Australia. When I asked my bank for help they made inquiries with their fraud section and told me it was all a scam and refused the request for a loan. I was shocked. I had already cancelled my trip to the outback after receiving the approval of my claim. I did not get a refund for the trip because it was too short notice and now I was about to lose most of my savings. I had renewed my passport and driver license in preparation for a trip to London.

I notified the barrister that I was not able to raise the transfer fee. He thanked me for my time. I tried to get help from the police. They could not help me because it was an international case and referred me to Interpol. I had to go to numerous security checks before someone talked to me. I didn't get any help there either because they claimed cases like that usually have a dead end in spite of the fact that I could provide them with names, addresses, and phone numbers. The British embassy was another place I contacted but they didn't take a case against their own country. It was a dead end for me. I felt very let down.

Just then my computer was corrupted and my telephone interfered with. I had to get my computer reprogrammed, a new telephone number, and a new visa card. If that was not enough, I was poisoned by chemspray from the air. My vegetables in the garden died and I broke out in terrible rashes. I received information on this spray from Cosmic Connection and a test was provided. The test proved positive for that poison.

I took a sample of the test and the information to the Royal Adelaide Hospital to make them aware of what was going on around us. They put me in the emergency ward for tests. When I was made to wait for ages from one test to the other, I wanted to go home and tried to leave.

I was stopped by security guards. I still tried to leave. I was agitated and tried to force my way out when I was surrounded by five security guards and returned to the ward. After they collected all my personal things—phone, radio, purse, pens, manicure set, business cards, mirror, comb, papers, and the chemspray report from Cosmic Connection, they transferred me to the psychiatric ward in the Repatriation Hospital. I was totally unprepared. I couldn't ring anybody because I didn't have my telephone book with me. I felt cut off from the world and didn't know what was happening.

I had had a powerful healing session with Kevin Robb from Cosmic Connection two months earlier and thought I was cured from bipolar and went slowly off my medication. I felt so good after his treatment (energy healing) but then so many things had happened to me and I had a relapse. I appealed against the detention but was unsuccessful.

The hospital opened a trust account for me with Public Trustees and my pension was paid into that account—against my will. I hadn't been contacted about that. It was totally unnecessary since I had no incoming bills at that stage and had arranged direct payments for my rent, telephone, and power.

I had to find out the hard way that the hospital was not prepared for emergency cases. It took nearly three weeks to get a toothbrush. Finally my landlord was notified where I was and my house manager brought me some of my clothes, which I had requested. They also sorted out the food in my home. A neighbour, who was the first to find out where I was, got a ladder from the neighbour across the road and climbed over my six-foot fence to water my backyard, another neighbour watered my front garden and collected the mail. They all knew how much I love my plants.

After three weeks, I was finally allowed to make some phone calls. That took a lot of pressure off me, but I had still to stay for another two weeks.

At last I could go home after a nurse was able to collect my belongings from the Royal Adelaide Hospital, where they were previously declared missing. It didn't give me much time to prepare for Christmas.

My psychiatrist notified the Public Trustee in December that I was capable of looking after my own affairs and my pension could be paid directly into my bank account again. Until then Public Trustee only collected my pension. They did nothing for me. After they received the notification, they did not release my pension into my bank account and sent me a cheque for $600 to pay for bills and living expenses. That amount didn't last long and I soon was in serious financial trouble. It took several phone calls and correspondence till my account was finally unwound from the Public Trustee in May, the following year.

However, I did have a wonderful party with my friends who had cared for me and my place while I was sick and I celebrated christmas with my son and my German friend and his partner. We watched Sydney's New Year's fireworks at night on television.

Not long before Christmas, my back pain returned. I had an x-ray taken, which revealed I had a fractured vertebra. A bone density test followed. The verdict was osteopenia in the spine and several joints. The doctor put me on a two-year plan with Actonel and vitamin D.

During December, a week after the first dose of actonel, I developed severe joint pains in my shoulders. I stopped actonel in January. By then the joint pains had spread to the right elbow, hips, and knees. A blood test for vitamin D showed normal results. At the end of February, I decided 'no more drugs for osteopenia', after a thorough research of other drugs for that purpose showed similar side effects. I was liable to attract the worst side effects.

I had a talk with the health minister—a friend of mine since the winery, where he was a customer—about my experience with actonel. He recommended getting a second opinion since I was only put on pain killers, which had hardly any effect. I sought another opinion in April. The doctor said he would not have put me on actonel and recommended treatment with calcium and fish oil supplements and ordered ultrasound for the most affected right shoulder. The pain in this shoulder made normal chores like dressing, combing my hair, reaching backwards, and lifting a real ordeal. He didn't want me to have too many x-rays. The diagnosis was bursitis. Treatment with herbal remedies was successful for the hips and knees but not for the shoulders.

In July, I agreed to cortisone injections in both shoulders. This treatment gave me my movements back but the pain persisted. It made me so angry that a pharmaceutical company was allowed to market such a dangerous product; it has worse side effects than mine (deterioration of the jaw). Bursitis is not on the side effect list, just joint pains, which could mean anything.

I decided I wanted to take the company on to stop the marketing of actonel and get compensation for my suffering. I contacted a lawyer. He wanted a report from my doctor that the bursitis was a side effect of actonel. My doctor referred me to two specialists. Neither of them would confirm this. They told me that no doctor would back me up on this because, I believe, they didn't want to get in trouble with the pharmaceutical company. When I told the doctor in another clinic that I wanted damage for my suffering, he noted in his report my past history with bipolar and hypertension, which had nothing to do with it. It seems that people with bipolar don't have the right to defend themselves. It meant, of course, I could not successfully pursue my case. The second specialist referred me to a local hospital for physiotherapy treatment, which did improve my condition.

In spite of all this, I had a wonderful seventy-fifth birthday party with my friends, who all lent a hand to make it a party to remember. It was to be my last birthday celebration as I didn't want to give my age away in the future even though most people said I looked ten years younger. We had strawberry punch, delicious continental finger food, cheese and fruit plates, black forest cake, and Pavlova accompanied by happy conversation and lots of laughs. Among my presents was a DVD—the first of a series about *Understanding the Universe*. When I watched it later I knew I had to get the series of thirty-six DVDs—one a month. It provided incredible information. My favourite was the DVD about the Hubble, but they were all fascinating and included the planets, galaxies, the space station, space pioneers, spacecraft and launchers, space missions, understanding the cosmos, and so on. The DVDs contained a little booklet about the contents with a test at the end for what I remembered of it. I faired well. It all filled my insatiable curiosity.

There were other ways to distract myself from my health problems and disappointments about the way things were going. My friend Raelene was successful with a job application as a counsellor in Victoria and needed someone to maintain the garden. I volunteered. The garden was pretty wild and needed a lot of work. I spent many hours there to control the weeds in the garden and ponds. I had a break when the pain wanted me to stop but I managed to change the picture considerably.

Joining the walking group from the Heart Foundation was a more leisurely distraction. I even won a shirt and a pedometer with my entry form. We walked along the beach for an hour every Friday morning, usually in excellent weather. The company in this group was always enjoyable. We had a break for stretches or rests and took in the wonderful views from the coastline, while talking about the history of the place, whale and dolphin watching, sunsets or travel experiences. The travel stories made an old dream of travelling to India, surface again.

Through attending an Indian evening, I met with a group which travelled regularly to India and turned their trips to unforgettable experiences. Unfortunately, their travel times never fitted into my diary, which led to another idea—encouraged by a lot of advertising from World Vision. I decided to sponsor a child in India. My request for a girl up to ten years old was not successful, but I thought I was on the right track to sponsor a child in need instead of travelling, which would give my life another meaning. Beside India, I felt a strong connection to Peru through the books from my German friend, and applied for a child in Peru, but again there was no girl in that age range listed. Instead, I found among 287 listed girls a lovely girl from Ecuador—next door to Peru.

Her name started with a German name and was followed by Spanish names, which had a musical sound to it. She was eight years old and lives with her mother and siblings in Esmeralda's Province. Her language is Spanish and her favourite games are role plays and imitation games. That's why I chose her. I love the Spanish language and music and think when a girl of her age is interested in role plays, she must be very intelligent and able to put herself into other people's life.

In her first letter she told me about her life and surroundings and that she wanted to be a doctor. I was really proud of her. She inspired me to want to go to Ecuador as a missionary or assistant to World Vision. I researched the possibilities of payments of my pension, living and travelling costs and accommodation in Ecuador. Centrelink would arrange payment of my pension into a bank account in Ecuador, which would enable me to live there independently, as living costs and accommodation are very cheap there.

When I discussed these possibilities with World Vision, they revealed to me that they don't have people from Australia working for them overseas. That was a hard blow. I did not understand that, especially since I was prepared to learn Spanish. Another disclosure from World Vision was about the way my money was spent. It didn't go to my sponsored child at all. It was paid into a pool and used to build infrastructure for the township. I was deeply disappointed. I wrote to World Vision to say that my money was meant for my chosen child's education. If they wanted money for infrastructure they should ask for other sponsorships. I felt it was false advertising when they put children in the window when they want money for infrastructure.

When they didn't agree to use my money for this child, I cancelled my sponsorship and wrote to her to explain why I did it. I assured her that she was very determined and would reach her goal to be a doctor anyway. I was informed she has another sponsor.

I needed something else to fill my life and started to write for the local newspaper *Coastal Views* under the headline Gems of the District about organisations I've been a member of and which played a vital role in the entertainment and education of people in the district, including the elderly. The U3A was the first, followed by Trees for Life, Friends of the Scrub, The Weekend and Coastal Capers, The Willunga Environment Centre—with their active involvement in the surrounding districts and vast education program and Friends of the Willunga Basin, who are fighting for the protection of the region from developers to keep the district a rural district and tourist attraction. Later, I wrote to the editor about the danger a desalination plant in our district would cause to the environment and the lifestyle of people on the coastline and visitors to the fishing spots when the brine was returned to the sea.

I stopped writing for the newspaper to be able to work on my autobiography, but I still had another outlet of my interests—I started a camera club in the U3A. I love photography but wanted to become more professional to be able to exhibit my photographs. I found a teacher for the club who had won several trophies for his work and was very enthusiastic about having his own club.

We advertised in the U3A newsletter and started with eight members. Our meeting place was in a lookout on the beach where we met armed with the camera, tripod, and a lot of expectations. We were pleasantly surprised by the professionalism of our teacher. He introduced us to digital photography, showed us how to get the best use from our cameras, gave us a glimpse into his own prize winning work, and sent us out to practise.

The results of our own work were shown at the next meeting. We also viewed his own DVDs at his home and had a session with models. I staged as a model because I was the most relaxed participant. It was all a lot of fun. Unfortunately, it ended because our teacher had too many other commitments and I couldn't find a replacement for him.

But it wasn't the end of my activities. I was still with the U3A and Cosmic Connection. At one meeting of Cosmic Connection, I found an invitation for a spiritual wellbeing weekend seminar on the information table. I felt a strong urge to attend and contacted the organiser. She helped me to solve my transport problem by contacting another participant to give me a ride.

A day before our departure there was an earthquake in the region where the seminar was to be held—a normally earthquake-free area. I saw that as a sign of importance for my trip. A very kind lady picked me up the next day, and we set off on a pleasant drive in beautiful weather through a lush green landscape. I learned that the lady was a music teacher and sound healer. It felt as though we had known each other a long time. We could talk about anything. It was a warm welcome to a meeting where I knew nobody.

When we arrived the next lady I met had a German accent. We immediately started a conversation. I was surprised how open-minded and friendly everyone was and felt instantly at home. This was totally unexpected. I received a warm welcome from the organiser who handed me the program and my name tag.

The aim of the get-together was to share our gifts, knowledge, and hearts in an atmosphere of non-judgement, fun, and love. The weekend did not have a particular theme—it was meant to increase the mind, body, emotional and spiritual health, and welfare. All beliefs which worked for the highest good were valued. We were asked to donate two hours of our time and for the remaining time receive from others.

I had no healing gifts to offer, so I signed up for kitchen duties at the registration. For me everything was new but the cooperation was inspiring. Everything went smoothly. Making new friends became very easy in this loving atmosphere. I had never met so many people in one spot with such friendly approach. There were sixty present.

While the first day was for getting to know each other, the program started with a welcome, followed by a heart-centred breathing meditation (the nine breath meditation) conducted by Mel, which everyone took part in. During the session I opened my eyes (we closed our eyes during the meditation) and saw a golden glow surrounding the mediator. I checked where the light was coming from. There was no sunlight entering the room and no electric light behind him. I was very curious. After the session I asked Mel what it was. He said, 'my energy'. I was puzzled and deeply moved. I felt very privileged that it was revealed to me. I found out later when I talked about it that no one else saw that, maybe nobody else opened their eyes. I knew Mel must be a very special person to be so gifted. It never left my thoughts. I could not remember the next session, a workshop about resonant nature, which was followed by painting mandalas. I had done many mandalas before but couldn't concentrate on one and painted a boat at sea instead. It was interpreted as me being on a voyage. I felt I was. My life seemed to head into a new direction.

After that I was brought back to reality with my kitchen duties for lunch. We were a happy group—heating and serving meals to which we had contributed to help to keep the costs down (it is a non-profit organisation). There were mainly vegetarian dishes (I made an exception, among a few others, with my potato salad with anchovies) and luscious cakes offered on self-serving tables. Everyone enjoyed the variety of foods.

The afternoon was set aside for universal and individual healings. I had sound healing with my newly-found German friend with a drum, bells, and other instruments. I had the feeling that the drum chased some of my fears away, which I didn't even know were there. While I was first startled by the louder sounds of the drum, I became totally relaxed after a while. The other sounds added to my relaxation. I felt in excellent spirit afterwards. The afternoon was closed with a sound healing with crystal bowls. The sound of crystal bowls is very powerful and took me into another dimension. The mentor, with long blond curly hair, was dressed in white and looked like an angel. It was a transforming experience.

After dinner, there was a heart chakra meditation for all, followed by entertainment in an open church on the hillside, where we played drums and other instruments by moonlight. I became a very enthusiastic drummer-I had never played a drum before. We simply celebrated being together in such beautiful surrounding with this wonderful atmosphere.

The next morning I arose early. Kitchen duties started at 7:00AM. I was the only one on the list and I started to worry but my prayer for help was answered. Gradually, quite a few helpers arrived and we managed to set out the table, cut the bread, and boil the eggs. Everything was ready in time. That was another proof of the spirit of cooperation.

The morning was filled with a session of tai chi and yoga. I chose yoga (my experiences with tai chi were pretty mixed). I have never tried yoga before. It was great fun. I did well, in spite of my stiff knees. The teacher involved everyone. We were sitting on cushions, but went up and down with the different exercises. I became well aware that I was the oldest in the class (actually, on the whole weekend), but I am used to that. I was the oldest in Cosmic Connection, too. I love the challenge with young people. They can teach us a lot.

By brunch time we finished the clean-up and packing. The weekend ended with a closing ceremony where we all stood in a circle and said our thanks to the organiser and people who made this weekend possible for us. I received many hugs and well wishes. The most memorable hug was given from Mel. I respected him highly and feel very honoured to find his friendship. The day ended with the news that a school of twenty sharks had passed by the Normanville coastline, an unusual event for me. I thought that was another important omen for this unique weekend.

Coming home was a surprising experience. I missed the group and my driver already. Even so things seem to be harmonious and welcoming. I was so grateful to have such a lovely home to come back to.

The year ended on a happy note with an outing to Adelaide with friends to watch the fireworks. It was spectacular and the music was great, too. We believed we even saw a UFO.

MEL

- -

Three weeks after the spiritual wellbeing weekend, I met with Mel at the Healers Market. I caught up with him in a quiet moment and we had a chance to talk. We were sitting on the podium, where he had his stand overlooking the commotion of the market. We unravelled some of our stories of our lives. We found we were both organic farmers—being very nature bound—only I had long-retired from farming and Mel was still running a hundred acre farm with vegetables.

When I asked Mel about his family, he admitted that life with the family was not easy as they could not follow his way of life. I told him about my illness (bipolar) and emphasised that I wished nothing more than being cured from it—silently being convinced he would be the only one I would trust to heal me. We arranged to have a session in my place.

We had the first session a day after Christmas. He came prepared with a folding bed, a case with crystals and coloured bands, candles, and Tibetan bowls. It was to be a memorable event with treatment under hypnosis, which has never been possible in my life before but was tried for alcohol abuse and bipolar by several of my doctors. I was fully conscious during the process, felt extremely relaxed, and had no wish to do anything—including moving. It was so beautiful that I found it hard to return to reality. Mel was very caring and he helped me off the bed and handed me a glass of water.

The session was all about getting to know me and programming me for a happy life with music, dancing, and feeling young. I felt enriched through the energy from the crystals which Mel placed under the bed and on my body along my energy fields (the chakras). The colour stripes played a role, too—each had a different meaning. It was an experience which had a strong impact on my life. It made me extremely joyful. We planned further sessions when Mel's time would allow it. We were both busy.

I met Mel again at another Healers Market. He greeted me with a big hug and we had another chance to talk although he was busy with clients in between. I had the feeling that Mel would play a big part in my life. We made arrangements for another session early in February.

In this session I experienced even deeper hypnosis. We went down my timeline through different events—not necessarily traumas—till we ended up with experiences in the womb. Apparently, my parents talked about a boy when they talked about the baby—me. It hurt. It was the seed of my inferiority complex.

Mel compared this discovery with a lake in a storm with very rough waves. He made them slowly go down till the lake became totally calm in a beautiful surrounding. The feeling went over to me. He erased the painful experience I had with that memory. I felt totally at peace, relieved, and free from my inferiority complex, which had haunted me all my life and I was sure was the cause of my illness and the basis of my interaction with the world. I always felt I had to prove myself.

My bipolar started when Harold died and I thought I was totally useless without him. Nobody loved me and I could not see a future for myself. My self-esteem was at the lowest level. All that has changed now and a brighter future lay ahead.

A happiness like never before came over me. We both felt we reached a huge achievement—and that in two sessions. I was sure I was cured. This would mean life without hospitals and medication—after thirty three years of control of the Mental Health Service. This seemed to be a miracle. But this time I wanted proof after the failure of Kevin's (leader of *Cosmic Connection*) healing session.

On our next meeting I asked Mel if he would dance with me. I can't dance with everyone, only when I have no inferiority complex. Mel, in my opinion, stood high above me with his education and spiritual experiences. However, we discovered earlier that we had an education in the same academies—Earth Star in West Australia, Learning Strategy in Minnesota, and the Academy for Future Science in Los Gatos-US, but Mel had done many more courses than me. He is also qualified in crystal resonance therapy, past life therapy, hands on intentional healing, massage, reiki and reflexology, and does agricultural lectures, crystal workshops, and nine-breath heart-centred meditation. If I could dance with Mel, I believed I didn't have an inferiority complex anymore.

I put some music on and Mel asked me for a dance with an elegant hand movement, which made me feel very honoured. We danced and became very close. For me that was proof that I was cured. My happiness had no boundaries. It was sheer bliss. I never knew what was missing in my relationships, but I know I found it in the friendship with Mel.

Well, happiness means different things to different people. It all depends on what you desire and have fulfilment of. Being well and doing well is the basis of great happiness. I achieved that through Mel. My financial security and living in a lovely place played a role, too. I don't need great wealth. I have no debts and no worries and fears. I have been told that my joy radiates to people around me.

I felt so good that I decided I wanted to go off my medication. This had caused high blood pressure to an extent that I had fainted four times and had been admitted to a hospital three times where cause of the fainting could not be established. I wanted to stop all that!

On the next appointment with my psychiatrist, we discussed my intention. She was very reluctant but finally agreed to a slow reduction of my medication with close monitoring. That's what I hoped for. I felt better with every smaller dose and used my increased energy for researching my autobiography and articles for the newspaper.

I gained access to my hospital records through 'freedom of information'. I had been warned by hospital staff not to read them. They feared they could trigger my illness again. I felt sure that would not occur and it didn't. Instead, I became annoyed about the way I have been judged. There was no understanding why I chose to get off my medication at times. Well, doctors did not suffer the side effects and constant control.

I read the records like a case history of somebody else. It is interesting how people see you when they don't make an effort to get to know you. It was always mentioned that I was neatly dressed. In some records I was described as restless or upset, but I never found an attempt of the staff to find out the reason for that or any guidance how to solve my problems.

In the records of Howard House I made an interesting discovery—my blood group was listed AB rh neg. It was diagnosed as B rh neg in Germany. My research of the blood group AB rh neg revealed that it is the rarest blood type in the world.

I didn't believe there was a mistake, rather, that a miracle might have occurred when I had the huge blood transfusion and the out-of-body experience in 1965. The records of that hospital stay have unfortunately been destroyed.

My research and the interviews for the newspaper went well. I learned more about the district and the involvement of the Willunga Environment Centre and Friends of the Willunga Basin. It was all very challenging.

Apart from that, I had more sessions with Mel. I am very curious about my past life history. Mel applied 'past life therapy' with deep hypnosis. The results were overpowering. After one session we were discussing the outcome when the immensity stopped us talking. We were holding hands for a long time-just sitting there with closed eyes and feeling our energies flowing through us. We became very connected.

I cannot go into the experiences in our sessions, they are confidential. Everyone would have a different and very personal experience if they undergo this therapy. It can only be done in a totally trusting, peaceful atmosphere. For people who like to try it, 'it feels sooo good!' I was transferred into another level of consciousness and felt very blessed.

When visiting the Healers Market again, I had a cup of coffee with Mel. On the way out I found a ring trodden into the ground. I lifted it up and saw it was quite beautiful—silver with a purple inlay with pairs of daisies painted on. One pair had a sun over it. It fitted my ring finger and I left it on.

A month later I noticed the ring had changed. It lost the inlay and looked like a wedding ring. It happened on the date of my wedding to Gabor, the twenty seventh of May. I would have loved to know the meaning of this. The twenty-seventh of May was often an important day in my life. It definitely had nothing to do with Gabor. He doesn't even communicate with me. I left the ring on as a sort of protection. I didn't want to meet someone else. At our next meeting we discovered that Mel was wearing the same ring as mine, with a loose twisted inlaid band. I would like to know the meaning of this coincidence.

The next weeks brought more life changing events. After my psychiatrist broke her promise that I could reduce my tablets every fortnight, Mel decided he would accompany me on the next visit to support my intention. My doctor agreed to stick to the original plan after some hesitation. It was a courageous decision on her part. She could be held responsible if I became sick again. We left her office in an elated mood and went for lunch and a stroll to the beach. People turned their heads wherever we passed. Our happiness must have shone.

I then received a surprise call from Melbourne. Manfred's family asked me if they could give my telephone number to my sister, Gerda, who had recently lost her husband and was living alone, too. They wanted us to be in contact again after over twenty years of silence. I agreed. Next day I had a call from her. It seemed that no time had passed. We clicked immediately and arranged a meeting at my place.

There was a big hug when she stepped off the bus. We started talking right away. The feelings of our childhood were rekindled. There was so much to talk about—our husbands, our separate life in Australia, our childhood. It never stopped. Our lips got dry from all the talking. We had to keep a water jug handy. What a day of discoveries it was.

We had many interests in common, did many things in the household the same way, and liked the same food. Gerda liked crystals, too. She gave me a crystal pendant and she had no idea that I was involved with crystals through Mel. I gave her an amethyst (her birthstone) out of my collection, which I had recently acquired. We really found each other like never before. We both wanted to stay connected and continue visiting each other.

At the same time I was preparing two photo exhibitions. I took some photos for them in a full moon night on the beach and in surrounding areas. After developing the film, I found orbs in the pictures. This greatly surprised me as I did not see them when I took the photos. They were clearly showing as a circle and circles with a rainbow around them. I became very excited. I was always hoping I would see them sometime and it became reality! I even took some daylight photos with them in the botanic garden and in my own garden. I felt very privileged. I had only seen them in photos in Cosmic Connection before. Now I was wondering what the reaction would be at the exhibitions. If the interest shown in these photos in a meeting of Cosmic Connection was anything to go by, they would become a great talking point.

This was not the only surprise. At this time I often saw lights in the sky which looked like they had wings and moved like UFOs, which changed colours from yellow to orange and red. I had seen UFOs before but never so many in such short succession. There were multiple recordings from other people at the same time about the sightings. I felt elated every time I experienced something like that. It looked like they were sending messages with the way they moved—unfortunately unintelligible.

While all this was happening, Mel started to get organised for a long-awaited four month's world trip to sacred places. To prepare me for his long absence, Mel suggested starting a crystal workshop in my place, which I was to carry on with informal meetings of people with similar interests in spiritual awareness. My interest in crystals stemmed from the treatment I had from Mel. I knew about the energies crystals vibrate into our bodies when placed on certain chakras and believe in their healing properties.

Crystals have been used for healing as long as we have existed as species. The first historical references of the use of crystals come from ancient Sumaria, where they were included in magic formulas. Stones were worn for protection and health. The ancient Greeks attributed a number of properties to crystals. Many names used today are of Greek origin. The word crystal comes from the Greek word for ice. It was believed that clear quartz was water—so deeply frozen that it remained solid.

Crystals have played a role in all religions. They are mentioned throughout the bible and the Koran. Many tribal cultures have continued to use gemstones in healing to this very day. In western countries, with the advent of the new age around 1980, the use of gemstones began to re-emerge as a healing method. Much of the practice was drawn from old traditions, with more information gained by experimentation and channelling. It is viewed as an acceptable complementary therapy offered as qualification subject—and it is a fascinating subject.

I was excited about Mel's plan and invited six friends to our first meeting. Mel brought another guest. The course was called Introduction to Crystal Resonance Healing. The aim was to increase the awareness of crystal intelligence. Mel had created a manual, which contained twenty-five crystals, their properties, and where to place them on the body, as well as an explanation of how crystals are formed and why they have powerful energy potentials.

Mel is so attuned to the crystals that he receives guidance and influence for the course of action. The crystals told him which ones wanted to come. They guided him further on how to arrange the room for the workshop and which particular crystals had to be placed below each participant's chair, prior to the people actually arriving.

When the visitors did choose a seat, it was revealed that the subconscious mind of every single person had matched their needs to choose to sit above the crystal that most helped them at that moment in their awareness and emotional state. The same applied to the crystal we were to choose from Mel's collection on the crystal table. This proved to be a very powerful way to demonstrate the power and wisdom of the crystals, and how our subconscious mind does attune to them.

The workshop proceeded to cover the information in the manual about which crystals have what effect and everyone had the opportunity to lie on the healing table and receive a short crystal healing session. Each person was able to contribute to another's healing, if they wanted to.

Some participants felt much supported in that safe and caring group and found great solace, peace, and healing in the workshop. For others, the process brought forward fearful issues or they resisted the treatment. This is an indication of the powerful ways that crystals motivate us to examine our issues and push us to do something about them.

We finished with a lovely meal and decided to meet for informal gatherings to keep in contact until Mel takes over the workshop again after his return.

Mel departed a few days later. The trip was going to take him to England (Stonehenge and other places), Paris, Los Angeles, Sacramento, Mt Shasta, Lake Tahoe, San Francisco, Lima, Mexico and Peru—a highly inspirational trip! I followed the route on the internet and with my atlas.

After his return, Mel told me about his lifting spiritual experiences and brought me some little rocks from sacred mountains. He was so impressed by the peaceful lifestyle in Peru that he decided to go back there soon to live and help with the organic agricultural advancement.

I needed a new journey for myself, too, after the success of the sessions with Mel. I did not believe that it was my calling to carry out healing the way Mel does. I don't know enough about crystals and healing methods and most of all, I think for healing like that that you need a gift, which comes from within and I don't believe I have that.

I learned since that hypnosis cannot cure bipolar but it can erase traumas which cause psychosis or depression. The cause of the illness may be found in the genes. In my case a genes test arranged by a naturopath found that genes which are supposed to produce **Folate** were malfunctioning. Lack of folate can cause mental illness. Genes cannot be replaced yet, but a remedy can improve stability of the illness.

For his recovery a patient also needs **support** for building up his self-confidence by encouraging his talents, pointing out his achievements, helping him find a new goal for giving him a **purpose** in life, which he may lack or hasn't got the confidence for.

* * *

I still have the desire to help people and share my happiness with them. To be able to do more than I can now, I would like to gain more insight in the aboriginal cultures because I feel certain that because of their long heritage their wisdom for life in general—including healing—is developed far beyond our understanding. I have learned through reading many books that it takes years of observing and listening to aboriginal people before they trust white people enough to reveal their secrets. In the circumstances of my life and at my age, I could not afford to go away for long periods.

Life has always been my teacher. I am now embarking on a new journey in my life under a brighter sun.

THE WRITER'S PROFILE

In the past twenty years new forms of autobiography have brought forward many strong voices, especially women's voices.

This story is such a voice, of one woman's life. Many rich threads are woven together: being a child in Germany in the second world war; a successful manager of large government projects; a young wife emigrating to Australia for a new start, and the hard work of starting the first organic winery, in the 1960s, in McLaren Flat, South Australia. Through these episodes there is the sadness of lost dreams, the heartbreak of losing new love and a new beginning, and the devastation of dealing with the severe difficulties of the onset of mental illness in the bipolar range.

This writer is always an agent in her own life: her courage and determination to keep making the most of every new day, even when shadows are cast across the sunlight, is an inspirational story. More than one woman's story, it also adds to the rich collection of personal stories which contribute to the history of South Australia.

www.ingramcontent.com/pod-product-compliance
Lightning Source LLC
Chambersburg PA
CBHW030251130626
46549CB00002B/484

9 7 9 8 8 9 3 5 6 7 4 4 1